The Tek-Gnostics Heresies

Tales of Wonder from the *Collective Conscious*

Jack Heart

Published by
Tek-Gnostics Media
POB 3174
Ashland, OR 97520

ISBN: 10: 0997063505
ISBN-13: 978-0-9970635-0-9

DEDICATION

This curious little volume is lovingly dedicated to my sprawling, sassy, bumbling, brilliant, dysfunctional, dynamic, dear family, both nuclear and extended. Your love and patience knows no bounds.

This collection has been driven by the works of Buckminster Fuller, Eckhart Tolle, James Joyce, John C Lilly, Joseph Campbell, Ken Kesey, Marshall McLuhan, Philip K Dick, Robert Anton Wilson, Robert Hunter, Terrance McKenna, Timothy Leary, Vernor Vinge, and all the rest.

Honorable mention goes to our chemists...
Dr Albert Hoffman, Owsley, et al.

CONTENTS

ACKNOWLEDGMENTS

The following compellation owes its existence to the work of the incomparable psychologist, Carl G Jung, PhD. Jung's foundational work on psyche, the collective unconscious and especially synchronicity, defines this author's understanding of humanity's relationship between the outer and inner worlds.

Finally, I wish to acknowledge the Wiki phenomena, especially *Wikipedia* and her myriad contributors. In this work, I have referenced Wikipedia, as well as other Wikis, as a source for additional information. I do so in the spirit of how modern humanity accesses and researches data in our aggregated, globally networked information age. Wikipedia is a prime example of what I refer to as the collective conscious.

PROLOGUE

"There is no heresy or no philosophy which is so abhorrent to the church… as a human being"

- James Joyce

Her•e•sy (hĕr´ĭ-sē) *Noun* …from the Ancient Greek αἵρεσις…"choice" or "thing chosen."

1. An opinion or a doctrine at variance with established religious beliefs, especially dissension from or denial of Roman Catholic dogma by a professed believer or baptized church member.
2. Adherence to such dissenting opinion or doctrine.
3. A controversial or unorthodox opinion or doctrine, as in politics, philosophy, or science.

- American Heritage Dictionary

I am essentially an optimist and yet I tend to be, by nature… suspicious. Consequentially, I suspect that to be born a human Earthling in this day and age is truly a wondrous thing. I suspect the profound mystery of being human resides in the relationship between man and universe. I suspect the profound beauty in being human resides in communication of this relationship. Further, I suspect that our being alive at this point in time is no coincidence.

As a practicing optimist, I imagine that optimism acts as a counterbalance to pessimism. Optimism aligns with creative universal powers, while pessimism allies with destructive forces. I suspect that these universal forces are at work in our world today and we, as sentient beings, periodically choose to align ourselves with one power or the other. This dualistic struggle is played out daily. However, it is in the choosing... in the exercising of our free will... that the spark of our divinity is demonstrated.

I consider these propositions to be mythologies. Mythologies such as religion and science help us to conceptualize our world. They become roadmaps that allow us to navigate the strange world we inhabit. Beliefs and mythologies are conceptual artifacts. Tools designed by humans to assist them in their navigation. Likewise, the book you now hold in your hands outlines new mythologies that were put into play in the decades following World War II.

It is no secret that the world in which we live today is a darker, more mysterious place than anyone could have imagined at the close of the twentieth century. Strange, new forces are at work... ancient powers arise, as if in response. This quickening evolution (some may contend: devolution) has dramatically "raised the stakes" for humanity. Traditional institutions of mind and spirit have proven corrupt in the face of such change.

These changes have forced me to reluctantly reconsider my imaginings of the way in which this world works, to the point of radicalism... to the point of heresy. I did not come to this heretical position easily or overnight. My path to heresy was a circuitous one. Let me explain...

I entered State College with every intention of pursuing a degree in journalism. I signed up for the requisite classes and embarked upon my academic odyssey as the autumn leaves began to fall. I soon found that my imagination and heart had been captivated... abducted, really... by the study of Archaeology. I became enamored with antiquity and artifact. Who were these ancients? ...and what mysteries influenced the foundation of civilization?

My youth and adolescence had been caught up in the gravity of the late sixties... my trajectory would slingshot around an orbit of the "Summer of Love." At State College, my thinking assumed the curiosity of the cultural anthropologist. At the weekend off-campus party for instance... why was marijuana ceremoniously passed around in a circle, in the living room... while cocaine was sequestered away behind locked doors? What cultural norms were being displayed? What ancient ritual was being repeated? People are strange, no?

Questions concerning substances of an illicit nature... stimulant or euphoric... paled in comparison to my introduction to LSD-25. Abruptly, the doors of perception were kicked in... undisputed belief in orthodoxy melted away. Magical realms, alien entities, a living, breathing, sentient universe became manifest. Like an imagined Steve Jobs... my mind was blown with psychedelic revelation. In retrospect, the ensuing computer revolution, facilitated by Jobs et al, was an obvious outcome of the psychedelic experience.

Steeped in the brilliant groundwork of such luminaries as Dr Carl Jung and Dr Albert Hoffman... standing on the shoulders of such rascally tricksters as Timothy Leary and Robert Anton Wilson... road tested from decades of personal exploration on the "high frontier" of inner space... I marveled, as a new techno cosmology began to emerge. The rise of personal computing had turned punk into cyberpunk. Fueled by the enthusiasm of the new information age, I, along with the rest of humanity, would turn the corner on the 20th century and get a first glimpse at the new millennium.

A handful of traumatic and tumultuous years later, facilitated by the Web 2.0, social media and the personal weblog revolution... I established an outpost on the perimeter of cyberspace, intending to chronicle the amazing cultural transformation that occurred during the first decades of the 21st century. This outpost took the form of a website: www.tekgnostics.com. Within Tek-Gnostics' virtual walls, all of the strangeness, the high weirdness, the mad illuminations of "Gnosis," infused with cyberpunk sensibilities... merged into a new electronic medium of mystery... residing within the world-wide-web.

Since its inception, the Tek-Gnostics network has grown into an archive of illuminated manuscripts for the digital age. Together, we explore the potentialities of our near future, as well as examine recent cultural events of our past, thereby focusing the present into succinct clarity. Here we gather... faces aglow... around the digital campfire, anticipating the ancient tales to be told once again...

Tek-Gnostics incorporates and utilizes a variety of cultural artifacts, some of which have religious connotations. Given the times in which we live, the connotations of such are evolving. Accordingly, what has been commonly considered religious artifacts, are presented in such a way as to be viewed as heretical in nature, by those who desperately cling to antiquated religious frameworks.

It has since become abundantly clear that religious institutions of the West have failed us in relevancy and vision. This is a generous assessment. Humanity has moved beyond such archaic analogies. Therefore a new vision... a new narrative... a new mythology arises to more accurately, more deeply describe our rapidly changing world.

The Tek-Gnostics system reaches to describe our evolving universe in the language of modern myth. This mythic system, as introduced in this book, utilizes psychological artifacts, drawing primarily from analytical psychology, as developed by Dr Carl Jung. Jung's ground-breaking work on archetypes, the collective unconscious and especially the concept of synchronicity... infuses and informs Tek-Gnostics. Consequently, you hold in your hands, the product of the aggregated esoteric experiment that began so many years ago. The book format allows these ideas to be more fully contemplated and expanded upon.

This compilation is not intended to be an exhaustive treatise on the subject, but rather an introduction to an evolving system of perception that merges technology (tek) with intuitively derived knowledge (gnosis). Consider this work to be a primer to the amazing changes taking place, as well as the forces at work that are rearranging our modern world. Although Tek-Gnostics issues from the perspective of history, I strive to tell her story as well. Make no mistake... Goddess (Gaia) is alive and magick is afoot!

Before moving on... a final note to the reader: It is no coincidence that you have chosen this exact moment to discover the *Tek-Gnostics Heresies*. This seeming happenstance is a function of synchronicity. This moment, like all things in our dualistic universe, is necessarily perfect. The journey toward a deeper understanding of what it means to be fully human begins anew daily... right here and right now.

So... with this most auspicious moment as a catalyst... let the journey begin...

1
SLOUCHING TOWARD SINGULARITY

*"And what rough beast... its hour come 'round at last...
slouches towards Bethlehem, to be born?"*

- W B Yeats

"Within thirty years, we will have the technological means to create superhuman intelligence. Shortly after, the human era will be ended."...So began Vernor Vinge's now-infamous presentation titled: *The Coming Technological Singularity: How to Survive in the Post-Human Era* ...at the VISION-21 Symposium held on March 30th, 1993. The event was sponsored by the NASA Lewis Research Center and the Ohio Aerospace Institute. The renowned science fiction writer, professor of mathematics (retired) and computer scientist went on to say...

"The acceleration of technological progress has been the central feature of this century. We are on the edge of change comparable to the rise of human life on Earth. The precise cause of this change is the imminent creation by technology of entities with greater than human intelligence. There are several means by which science may achieve this breakthrough...

1) There may be developed computers that are "awake" and superhumanly intelligent. To date, there has been much controversy as to whether we can create human equivalence in a machine. But if

5

the answer is "yes, we can", then there is little doubt that beings more intelligent can be constructed shortly thereafter.

2) Large computer networks and their associated users may "wake up" as a superhumanly intelligent entity.

3) Computer/human interfaces may become so intimate that users may reasonably be considered superhumanly intelligent.

4) Biological science may provide means to improve natural human intellect.

Decades have passed since those prophetic words were spoken at the VISION-21 Symposium. Today, all four of Vinge's scenarios seem at least viable, if not inevitable. Currently, computer driven artificial intelligence (AI) has progressed to the brink of Vinge's impending technological singularity, as suggested in item one above. Advances in Deep Learning (a branch of machine learning, using sets of algorithms that attempt to model high-level abstractions) bring artificial neural networks ever closer to human parity.

Our modern internet, accessed via smart phones, tablets and a multitude of operating system's browsers... cumulatively networked and referred to as the world-wide-web... looks suspiciously like item two. Likewise, the trans-human movement or transhumanism, is a near perfect fit to item three. Lastly, recent work being done with the human genome project and continued DNA research on more refined, next-generation neuroenhancing drugs, as dramatized in Neil Burger's 2011 Film: *Limitless* ...are reasonable representations of item four.

Simply stated, Vinge's technological singularity is the moment when machine intelligence surpasses human intelligence. Although this proposition is frightening to many, it is humanity's evolutionary and technological success that has brought us to this crossroads. Even as our computer networks gain more (human-like) ability and assume more complex responsibilities, humanity continues to evolve greater capacity.

If an AI or a computer network becomes sentient and thus capable of intelligent self-reflection... if that artificial self awareness is comparable in sophistication to that of a human... humanity too must move beyond our present (perceived) limitations. Similarly to AI, humanity must move beyond our current capabilities. We too must cross our own human-singularity threshold.

Paranormal: the New Normal

Throughout history, there have been many individuals who possess extra-ordinary capabilities. Up to this point, these abilities have been viewed with fear and skepticism. In the distant past, these attributes were considered magical or mystical. More recently, these exceptional human faculties have been labeled... paranormal. In regard to human capability, the word Paranormal has become a generic term that designates human experiences that are indicative of phenomena considered to be outside of science's current ability to explain. The reality is... the abilities of these afore-mentioned extraordinary individuals... what has been popularly labeled paranormal... are not out of our reach, they are rather... our inheritance.

Taking the evolutionary next step, crossing the human-singularity threshold requires humanity to fully embrace these capabilities that have historically been considered paranormal by the general populace. In a world of globally networked AI, what has heretofore been labeled paranormal must become the new normal. Human capability must evolve beyond our current limitations, if for no other reason than to anticipate and prevent a "Rise of the Machines" nightmare scenario, as popularized by the Terminator film franchise, from actually coming to pass. Regardless of the likelihood of this scenario, we have to stay smarter than our machines, folks.

Staying ahead of the machines is not only an increasingly evident challenge of the 21st Century; it is fast becoming a prerequisite for the survival of our species. For humankind, Singularity is less of a technological crisis than it is an existential one. We must, at the very least, preserve and maintain parity with our technological creations, for the sake of our evolving humanity. So too must we keep a handle on the "high weirdness" that is our Brave New Future. What was once considered fringe theory is fast becoming reality... as the paranormal morphs into the new normal.

Such is the nature of the new paradigm...

Artifacts & Mysteries

Modern humanity has been successful as a species for two fundamental reasons: First... our ability to create and manipulate tools or artifacts and second... our apparent rapid intelligence increase that occurred over the last 10,000+ years, as evidenced by the archaeological record. For better or worse, these two interrelated attributes gave rise to the myriad of civilizations and cultures that have supported our species' nearly inconceivable success. Our collective proto and true human ingenuity had enabled us to devise not only wondrous material artifacts, beginning over two million years ago with stone tools... but more recently, conceptual artifacts as well.

Conceptual artifacts that have been integral to our species-wide success and advancements include symbolic communication such as music, art, language and writing. The archaeological record indicates the emergence of symbolic expression, such as the cave paintings found in the El Castillo cave in Cantabria, Spain, dating back some 40,000 years. True writing, such as cuneiform, found in ancient Sumer, emerged approximately 6,000 years ago. With continued investigation, modern archaeology pushes back the recognized timeline of modern man's anthropological advancements, to ever-earlier dates. Again, this "explosion" of intelligence and technology over the span of the last 10,000 years was not only phenomenal, it was all but unbelievable... and very mysterious.

Ancient Hindu scripture spoke of a grand cycle of universal creation and destruction, composed of four "ages" or Yugas.[1] These four ages cycle from a high Golden Age, called the "Satya Yuga" ...through the Tetra and Dvapara Yugas, to a Dark Age (our current Yuga), known as the "Kali Yuga." The Roman Poet Ovid[2] also spoke of the four ages of man... the Golden Age, Silver, Bronze and finally the Iron Age. As with the Hindu cycle, each successive age represents a significant degradation of the human condition.

Conversely, contemporary Archaeological ages progressed from the Stone Age (which ended circa: 6,000 BCE) to the Bronze Age (circa: 3,000 BCE) through the Iron Age (circa: 1,000 BCE) to our

---

[1] see: https://en.wikipedia.org/wiki/Yuga
[2] Publius Ovidius Naso (20 March 43 BC – AD 17/18), known as Ovid, was a Roman poet best known for the epic: Metamorphoses.

modern age. From this perspective, the modern age rapidly transitioned from the agricultural age, through the industrial age, the space age and most recently... the information age. Each successive era's timeline and technological progress accelerated exponentially from the preceding one.

Unlike the ancient's grand cycle of the ages, the contemporary vision of the ages is one of accelerated and uninterrupted advancement (which, as we will examine later, may or may not be true). Again, the archaeological record indicates that modern man has been present on earth for more than 200,000 years. Returning to the miraculous technological ascendancy of humanity over the last 10,000 years, this explosive rise is suspicious, to say the least. It is as if humanity had been somehow assisted in our rise.

What follows is a series of investigations into the mysterious nature of humanity's amazing rise to planetary prominence. We seek to identify any catalyst that may have existed in association with that rise. Humanity's astounding blending of technology and intelligence and our ability to create, utilize and communicate this knowledge will also be a primary focus of our explorations. For it is in the attributes of creation and communication that humanity's past success... and future survival... depend.

It is a strange world we live in... and the truth is far stranger than fiction. The wide-spread acceptance and development of so-called paranormal ability or "Psi" phenomena, is what will keep us one step ahead of the machines. Our challenge, as a species, is to evolve and grow by cultivating these paranormal abilities, such as extra-sensory perception, pre-cognition and telekinesis. These dubious sounding abilities are in fact routinely experienced daily by all of us. Daydreaming of an acquaintance, only to have them unexpectedly call or text you on your mobile, is but one small, mundane example of such emerging phenomena.

Our challenge is in fact two-fold. It is not enough to simply cultivate these paranormal abilities. We must also demonstrate the requisite wisdom to intelligently manage our evolving capabilities. This wisdom will entail a subtle shift of perspective, as to what these paranormal abilities are and where they came from. It is through the fusion of capacity and understanding that the transition to the new normal is made possible.

As we move forward, our two-fold existential challenge is to navigate our rapidly evolving future, while preserving our humanity. We must grow into the twenty-first century... the "Century of Singularity" ...with competence and grace. We must learn to balance the outer world of materialism and technology, with the inner world of consciousness and spirit. In so doing... we improve upon the likelihood that our own technologies, our own creations... will not forsake us.

2
A VISION OF THE FUTURE

"The future belongs to those who give the next generation reason for hope."

- Pierre Teilhard de Chardin

We stand... poised upon a precipice of unfathomable consequence. We nonchalantly name this precarious moment, the ground beneath our feet: "the present." That vast expanse that we call "the past" unfolds beneath and behind us like an immense nightmarish plain, stretching to infinity. The nexus of possibilities that lay before us, caught up in the gravity of eternity... collectively known as "the future" ...is obscured. It is occluded by a fog of potentialities... influenced... facilitated in part by the amazing, synchronistic events that were put into play in our past.

The first decade of the 21st century had been quite a ride. The transition from the old paradigm to the new millennium began abruptly on September the Eleventh, 2001. On that day, with the orchestrated demolition of the World Trade Center and other violent acts, the citizenry of Spaceship Earth[3] awoke to a "brave new age." Broadcast live around the world by a (then) pervasive media machine, this new age came crashing into our living-rooms via television... that "luminous screen of mediocrity." Little did we know at the time,

---

[3] See: https://en.wikipedia.org/wiki/Spaceship_Earth

11

that this televised spectacle was to be the "last hurrah" of "pre social media broadcasting."

As the cameras rolled, the world watched, transfixed. This was not the new age that many of us visualized in yoga class. This was not the new age we envisioned during the "Harmonic Convergence." This was not even the imagined future hinted at by the Y2K scare. This was a darker wake-up call that viciously "came up-side" our collective head as if to say… "Welcome to the future, chump."

Consequently, our shared vision of the world in which we live, was greatly influenced by the events of that infamous day. 9/11 is as consequential to us as Pearl Harbor was to the "Greatest Generation." Seemingly overnight our planet's socio-economic landscape had been re-arranged into a mix of multi-nationalism and archaic tribalism. Corporate powers, favoring their shareholders interests over National sovereignty, systematically stripped or "hollowed" National governments of their once-pervasive authority to effectively govern. Meanwhile, a "Jihad" or holy war had been declared against capitalism in general and the Western World's neo-empirical expansionism in particular.

For decades leading up to 9/11, a "crusade" of Western interests had descended upon the Islamic world, most notoriously (and militarily) Kuwait, Yemen and Lebanon. Little wonder that there would be push-back from neo-conservative factions within Middle Eastern countries such as Iran. Little wonder there would be refuge for such, in lawless territories like Waziristan (the mountainous tribal region on the border between Afghanistan and Pakistan). The so-called Arab Spring aside, ultra-conservative fundamentalism, from all of the Abrahamic Desert Religions: Judaism, Christianity and Islam… East and West, seemed to hold disproportionate sway over the affairs of man.

Terrorists… Crusaders… Fanatics… Infidels…

Presently, a murky, slightly sinister haze obscures a clear view of our near future, making prediction difficult and more than a little fuzzy. Terrorism and covert operations have replaced diplomacy as a political first option. Even as terrorist cells get their footing here at home and around the world, traditional global economic mechanisms are breaking apart. We now find ourselves living in a post rule-of-law, "spy-vs-spy" world.

In the ensuing years since 9/11, the citizenry of the United States has witnessed an erosion of their civil liberties at the hand of the Military Industrial Complex 2.0 (aka: the Terrorism Industrial Complex) …commonly referred to as: "Homeland Security." The rapid growth of what authors Dana Priest & William M. Arkin have called Top Secret America: "began with an impulse to secrecy and a blank check from the US Congress in the days following 9/11. The Terrorism Industrial Complex now employs over a million people at 1,900 private companies and 1,300 federal organizations. This gargantuan intelligence counter-terrorism industry continues to virally expand with virtually no governmental oversight."

The combined impact of the Military Industrial Complex (MIC) and the more recent Terrorism Industrial Complex (TIC) has drastically impeded traditional governmental oversight. The MIC and the TIC has since merged into a massive hybrid bureaucracy composed of governmental and private sector entities. This amalgam of private, military and security interests has effectively mutated into a feral corporate police state… simultaneously hollowing traditional governmental oversight, while replacing it with a "Shadow Government" …what conspiracy theorists have called: the Deep State.[4] This so-called Deep State now dictates… unimpeded… US interests at home and abroad.

Recent revelations of the nefarious exploits of the US National Security Agency has brought the Deep State out of the shadow of conspiracy theory, into the light of mainstream public knowledge. International police actions… … levels of mass surveillance never before imagined, combine with the threat of domestically targeted surveillance drones… now bring us to the brink of a "global" corporate/police government that makes George Orwell's[5] vision of the future simultaneously darkly prophetic and strikingly understated.

Foreign intrigues perpetrated by our government, along with the outright lies told during congressional oversight hearings by high-ranking officials of the US security apparatus… cross the boundary from immoral to illegal. Such is the desperate (as usual) situation we find ourselves in, as we have collectively moved… half blind… into the 21st century.

---

[4] See: https://wikispooks.com/wiki/Deep_state
[5] See: https://en.wikipedia.org/wiki/Nineteen_Eighty-Four

It is a startling and sorry state of affairs to suddenly "wake up" to the realization that what we once euphemistically considered the "Land of the Free" has become the most incarcerating nation in the developed world. Contemporary America increasingly and horrifically resembles the "Evil Empire" that the 40th U. S. President, Ronald Regan famously charged the Soviet Union with, back in 1983.

Surviving the Brave-New-Age

The rise of the Deep State is not without push-back from the American citizenry, however. Sensing a shift of power, a general distrust of an increasingly hollowed out and impotent Government and a particular disgust for said Government's legislative branch… has steadily grown in the hearts and minds of many Americans. The seeds of popular uprising have found fertile ground with the likes of the Tea Party[6] movement, germinating on the political Right… and the Occupy[7] movement, squatting on the Left.

To illustrate the current socio-political climate surrounding our increasingly dysfunctional government, let us focus upon and contrast the reaction of two recently popularized fringe groups that have emerged within the mass-media landscape that is contemporary American culture…

One such group has been popularly referred to as the "Prepper" or survivalist movement, by American network television. The contrasting group has been labeled the "Community Resilience" movement by the American press. These two factions pursue very different agendas, both driven by the same macro-political climate mentioned above.

The survivalist camp has been growing over the past several decades and includes such factions as the militia movement, wilderness survivalists and proponents of the second amendment and "right to bear arms" movement. Recently, the American entertainment media-machine had "climbed on board" the survivalist bandwagon when National Geographic Channel aired: *Doomsday Preppers*. This popular reality show aired for 4 seasons, causing serious conspiratorial speculation and debate when it was cancelled after the 2014 season.

---

[6] See: https://en.wikipedia.org/wiki/Tea_Party_movement
[7] See: https://en.wikipedia.org/wiki/Occupy_movement

Within the survivalist camp, extreme Right and Left wings are represented by the likes of Posse Comitatus[8] and Earth First![9] It could be argued that the radicalism of the National Rifleman's Association (NRA) and the conservative libertarianism of the Tea Party can be traced back to the survivalist mentality that was incubating in the late sixties and early 70's, emerging into public view in the 80's.

A neo-conservative faction of this collective continues to grow in popularity. The recent revival in extreme right-wing conspiracy theories... what the Southern Poverty Law Center[10] has called "Patriot Paranoia" has proliferated since the election of America's first Black President, the 44th U. S. President, Barak Hussein Obama. Xenophobic ramifications aside, the sentiment that is fed by these assorted conspiracy theories, creates an ever increasing distrust of the American Government. A certain amount of skepticism is healthy... the question is... how much is too much? At what point does mistrust become crazy?

Its critics suggest that the survivalist camp is fueled by "fear based" sentimentality. They charge that there appears to be an entropic, not enough to go around, survival of the fittest attitude that promotes a defensive posture, including the caching (hoarding) of provisions and weaponry. This mentality operates on the principle of scarcity. Survivalists feel the need to "protect what's mine." In the minds of its critics, the question arises... when does a defensive posture turn offensive? At what point do the defenders become predators?

Coinciding with the popularity of the Doomsday Preppers, another movement has recently emerged and been reported on by the more liberal press. Responding to similar concerns, the Community Resilience movement seeks to mitigate a perceived erosion of American national infrastructure. If it is true that the United States is going to "hell in a handbag," the "Resiliencers" (just coined this phrase... new hashtag perhaps?) seek to fill the void, created by an increasingly dysfunctional and retreating federal government... with home grown self-sufficiency.

The Community Resiliency camp can trace its modern roots back

---

[8] See: https://en.wikipedia.org/wiki/Posse_Comitatus_(organization)
[9] See: https://en.wikipedia.org/wiki/Earth_First!
[10] See: https://www.splcenter.org/

to the 70's, vis-à-vis the "back to nature" movement. It loosely includes such diverse factions as master & organic gardeners, alternative energy (solar, wind & hydro) or "off the grid" enthusiasts, the environmental movement and even natural childbirth advocates. Both Right and Left political ideologies are represented. Everyone from open source war strategist and former USAF pilot in special operations, John Robb, to Hippy media entrepreneur and futurist, Stewart Brand.

The Resiliency movement is rapidly gaining ground to the point of critical mass within the consciousness of the American public. This localized, yet networked response to diminishing services, crumbling infrastructure and lack of political will to fund such services, also speaks to an increased mistrust of government. More specifically, it speaks to skepticism over the government's ability to continue to deliver such services. "Resiliencers" operate from an extropic, "we can do anything we set our minds to" mentality. This philosophy also resonates with rural dwellers such as ranching and farming communities, as well as the more under the radar sub-culture of marijuana or "ganja growers" (still illegal in some States!).

As a non-obtrusive and primarily non-militaristic movement, the resilient community attracts less criticism. Its approach is mainly one of optimism and expertise. This mentality operates on the principle of abundance. It is an open, innovative and creative solution to the very serious challenges facing us all. The Resiliency movement is typified by its advocates as a "strength based" strategy that instills self-reliance within one's home and community. Growing food, generating local power and providing local manufacturing all promote economic stability within the home, the neighborhood, the community and the bio-region.

The question becomes… which of these two movements makes more sense as we move into a shared brave-new-future? On the one hand, the survivalists seek to address active security… as in providing paramilitary protection for their community and cached resources/provisions for their loved ones. Additionally, there is a desire to protect constitutional rights… specifically the second amendment right to bear arms and fourth amendment right against unreasonable search and seizures. This position appears to be confrontational…

"Keep the hell away from our personal freedoms and our god-given liberties, thank you very much."

On the other hand, the Resiliencers seek to address the passive security (self-reliance) question by building localized infrastructure, thereby decreasing dependence on the centralized state. They seek to meet their needs locally, not relying on international & interstate commerce, especially interstate freight delivery via semi-trucks. This speaks to a larger desire to end reliance on big government and big oil... i.e. international energy commerce. This position appears to be dismissive...

"We no longer need your artificially propped up international capitalism, thank you very much."

Time will tell in the long run, which is the wiser choice... "Prepper" survivalism or Community Resiliency. Active security is important, but at the end of the day... real and sustainable security is created by real and sustainable self-sufficiency. The immediate and essential choice before us is one of vision and intention. Before we can create a better future, we must first dream it... visualize it. This is not so much a question of: how do we get there? ...but a question of: who do we want to be, both individually and as a community... in getting there? Do we move into the future with compassion and integrity? ...or does the end justify the means?

It is important to bear in mind that both of these factions grew out of a dissatisfaction of the political status quo. The socio-political trend, typified by these factions, indicates the un-sustainability and splintering of our global economy, and a return to regional and local socio-economic organization. The extreme result of this trend may lead to the reemergence of the City-State. The rise in prominence of metropolitan mayoral incumbents who achieve national level recognition is but one early indicator of this trend.

Perhaps each faction has something to learn from their counterpart. Perhaps these seeming opposites are merely bookends. In truth, there is little difference between the ideological far-right and far-left. Their extremism and methodologies seem more similar than not. Regardless, the future we choose is the future we get.

Ultimately, the similarity between these two seemingly opposite factions may be found in their common roots. The genesis of both groups, appear to issue from that tumultuous time in American history, known to us today, simply as… "The Sixties." In fact, the fabric of much of our modern world can be traced back to that pivotal period in American history.

The libertarianism of the Tea Party, the collectivism of Occupy, the anarchy of the Earth First! …even the second amendment advocates owe their beginnings to movements, both political and cultural, that began in the sixties. It is ironic to note that the second amendment faction owes its contemporary founding to none other than that notorious sixties political action group: the Black Panthers.[11] Important social issues such as racial equality, gender equality and political parity, cumulatively "came to a head" in the 1960's.

Viewed through the lens of popular or "pop" media, the sixties are best remembered for the explosion of cultural expression, psychedelic experimentation and consciousness expansion known as the "Summer of Love." The events that played out in the summer of 1967 were a culminating flash point that was ignited by pressures which began to build at the close of World War II. The Summer of Love signaled the end of the old paradigm and suggested the beginning of the so-called "new age."

---

[11] See: https://en.wikipedia.org/wiki/Black_Panther_Party

3
THE RISE OF POP CULTURE

"People today are still living off the table scraps of the sixties. They are still being passed around... the music and the ideas."

- Bob Dylan

During those early post-war years, something new was germinating... unnoticed, almost lost in the outward expressions of the era. National optimism was at a peak during the 1950's. Even with the technological muscle of post-WWII America, there still lingered a collective innocence reminiscent of the last century. However, something strange was brewing in the psyche of the Western World... a fundamental shift... as yet undefined.

In the early 60's, communications theorist Marshall McLuhan prophesized that the visual, individualistic print culture would soon be brought to an end via an "electronic interdependence" ...where electronic media would replace the now-antiquated print culture. In this new age, humankind would move from individualism and fragmentation to a collective identity, with a "tribal base." McLuhan labeled this new social organization: *The global village.*

Key to McLuhan's theory was the idea that technology has no moral disposition. It is an artifact that deeply shapes an individual and his/her society's self-conception and self-awareness. As if in anticipation of the World Wide Web, McLuhan coined and popularized the usage of the term "surfing" to refer to rapid, irregular and multidirectional movement through a voluminous body of documents or knowledge.

In 1964, McLuhan published: *Understanding Media: The Extensions of Man*. In that work, McLuhan coined the phrase: "The medium is the message" …illustrating that a specific medium (print, radio, television, social, etc.) becomes an inseparable and influential part of the message being communicated. This symbiosis of media and message influences how the message is perceived. McLuhan's work implied that modern media itself was fast becoming more important than the content it carried. McLuhan brilliantly foresaw that a specific medium affects society, not only by the content delivered over the medium, but also, and most importantly, by the attributes of the medium itself.

In 1967, the very year of the Summer of Love, McLuhan published his "opus magnum," what would become his definitive work: *The Medium is the Massage*. Given that McLuhan was known to enjoy a good play on words, he adopted the word "massage" to denote the effect each medium has on the human sensorium (the sum of an individual's perceptions), taking inventory of the "effects" of numerous media in terms of how they "massage" the sensorium. To wit:

"Instead of tending towards a vast Alexandrian library, the world has become a computer, an electronic brain, exactly as (in) an infantile piece of science fiction. And as our senses have gone outside us… Big Brother goes inside. So, unless aware of this dynamic, we shall at once move into a phase of panic terrors, exactly befitting a small world of tribal drums, total interdependence, and superimposed co-existence.

Terror is the normal state of any oral society, for in it everything affects everything… all the time. In our long striving to recover (for the Western world), a unity of sensibility and of thought and feeling we have no more been prepared to accept the tribal consequences of such unity than we were ready for the fragmentation of the human psyche by print culture."

- Marshall McLuhan

As the sixties drew on, pop media began to evolve, mirroring McLuhan's ideas. Artists, such as Peter Max and Andy Warhol began producing psychedelic-neon-infused works of art that foreshadowed the luminous artwork of the coming information age. The US East

Coast music scene smoldered with avant-garde experimentalism as exemplified by Warhol's favored: *Velvet Underground,* whose work would inspire the punk scene of the late 70's and early 80's. Meanwhile, musical groups on the West Coast, such as the *Byrds,* the *Jefferson Airplane* and the *Warlocks* (aka: the *Grateful Dead),* were busy creating an accompanying psychedelic soundtrack for the culminating Summer of Love.

Perhaps one of the most profound musical vehicles of the emerging psychedelic Summer of Love, was epitomized and imported to American shores by that neo diasporic[12] phenomenon known as the "British Invasion". The musically driven cultural artifact in question was released in June of 1967, in the form of a record album titled: *Sgt. Pepper's Lonely Hearts Club Band* ...by Britain's master magicians... the Beatles. One of, if not "the" first concept album... *Sgt. Pepper* incorporated visually rich montage album art and auditory memes of the era, to produce the definitive multi-media musical offering of the decade.

Track three on the album: *Lucy in the Sky with Diamonds* ...was broadly considered a thinly-veiled reference to the chemical catalyst... the apex... the crown chakra of experience that fueled the Summer of Love... LSD-25. Championed by that rascally trickster, John Lennon (1940 to 1980), the Beatles foreshadowed and encapsulated the psychedelic revolution that was to come...

> *"Picture yourself in a boat on a river...*
> *With tangerine trees and marmalade skies.*
> *Somebody calls you, you answer quite slowly...*
> *A girl with kaleidoscope eyes."*

-from *Lucy in the Sky with Diamonds* by Lennon & McCartney

Looking nostalgically back on those tumultuous times, many of the "more seasoned" readers among us, may have spent hours of their fab-four-fan youth, scrutinizing Beatles album covers. As many of you, dear readers, no doubt recall... Paul was dead and the *powers that be* were hell-bent to cover it up. The remaining Beatles however, were busy encrypting secret messages in their music and on album

---

[12] See for example:
https://en.wikipedia.org/wiki/Music_of_the_African_diaspora#United_States

covers, trying to warn us.

Rumors circulated within the pop media world that Paul had been killed in a car-crash in January of 1967. In (conspiratorial) fact... it was widely reported that if one were to play the song: *Revolution 9* (from their 1969 White Album) backward... the message: "Turn me on, Dead man" could clearly be heard. Indeed, these early armchair investigations into Paul's death may have been many of your (dear readers!) first emersion in the world of conspiracy!

In order to fully appreciate the truly earth changing and epoch ending importance of the events of the Summer of Love, we must examine in greater detail, those events in history that lead up to this pivotal decade. As we shall see, the psychedelic sixties did not suddenly emerge out of thin air, after WWII. In fact, the emergence of the sixties' psychedelic culture is but one contemporary example of what anthropologists call an: entheogenic sub-culture, the lineage of which has a long, archaic history.

There were however, strange clues that surfaced after WWII that not only shed light on this emerging global psychedelic culture... they also tied in the converging trends of the occult and the paranormal. Again, the evolution (if not revolution) that played out in the summer of 1967, was ignited by pressures which began to build at the close of World War II. The Second World War demonstrated the horrors that humanity was prepared to visit upon each other and the planet.

The rise of industry... the industry of war... became a harsh reality in the waging of World War II. Although World War I demonstrated the horrific potential of technologies of modern warfare, such as the use of chemical weaponry, it was the Second World War that proved there was "no going back." Any hope of a return to a pastoral existence on planet Earth was forever eliminated by the mushroom clouds over Hiroshima and Nagasaki.

Mostly hidden by the emergence of the post-WWII industrial war machine, there emerged other "psychic signals" that foretold of a rise in the new paranormal. During the war, reports surfaced of "extreme interest" by Hitler's elite paramilitary corp., the *Schutzstaffel* (nefariously known as the SS) ...in paranormal artifacts and sacred sites, located around the planet. Rumors spread of their attempts to harness the "psychic energies" of these sites and artifacts.

Other subtle signals took the form of reports of strange flying balls of light that often accompanied allied and axis fighter and bomber planes. These aberrations became known as "Foo Fighters." Although many strange lights have been reported throughout history, the Foo Fighter foreshadowed that which was to become the UFO phenomena that would dominate mainstream media for decades to come. These and other strange phenomenon seemed to not only peak, but converge... congeal... in the years immediately following World War II.

The reality that there was no going back to a pastoral existence on planet Earth was evidenced by the abrupt global evolution of Earth's mythologies after WW II. Suspiciously similar to ancient myths, ala Sumer & Egypt, the earth spirits of farm and field rapidly began to transform into technologically driven celestial deities. Old Earth's "Leprechauns" were about to meet the "Little Green Men."

On June 24, 1947, pilot Kenneth Arnold claimed he had spotted a string of nine, shiny unidentified flying objects, flying past the Pacific Northwest's Mount Rainier. This was the first post-war sighting in the United States of the Foo Fighter phenomena that subsequently attracted nationwide news coverage. Thus began the modern era of "unidentified flying objects" or UFO sightings. Arnold's vivid description of the objects quickly led to the national press's coining of the terms "flying saucer" and/or "flying disc," which quickly became popular descriptive terms for UFOs.

As mentioned above, ancient civilizations such as those from Sumer and Egypt, whose myths informed later cultures, had developed robust celestial cosmologies of humanity's creation and evolution. In these mythologies, gods would descend from the heavens to impart divine guidance upon humanity. These deities were often portrayed by the ancients as flying or winged sun discs. As such, they are characterized as "solar deities" by modern archaeology.

The Foo Fighters of WW II and subsequent UFO/flying saucer phenomena of the 1950's abruptly modernized these ancient flying disc mythologies. Emerging rocket science of the Nazi regime brought with it a global faith in the power of technology. Technology quickly replaced magic... scientists and engineers replaced the high priests... extra-terrestrials replaced angels and demons. The winged sun discs of old became metal-hulled flying apparatus or "space ships."

From the ashes of WW II Nazi Germany emerged modern

rocketry and the resulting aerospace industry. These technologies, only hinted at before WW II, became a global certainty after the war. Post WW II earth saw an amazing rise in the technologies of modern industry. With these technologies came the unquestioned confidence in earth's newest mythic religion... Science.

As we shall see, the parallel re-emergence of psychedelic culture during this time, along with renewed interest in the paranormal, suggest that these synchronistic events arose organically, in tandem or "as if in response" to the rising power of technology. That the realm of the psychedelic would re-emerge in the modern world via the scientific discovery of the chemical compound, LSD-25, only strengthens the mythology that psychedelia re-arose when it did, as a counter-balance to technology. It is as if the ascension of the psychedelic experience arose as a cure... an inoculation... to the viral growth of technology...

In our next chapter, we will examine more closely these and other macro-trends that would lay the groundwork for a new global mythology. This innovative world view would forever put to rest the angels and demons of old. The emerging modern myths would replace superstitious old-world folktales of the fairy folk with... something new.

4
CARGO CULT

"Human history has become too much a matter of dogma taught by 'professionals' in ivory towers as though it's all fact. Actually, much of human history is up for grabs. The further back you go… the more that the history that's taught in the schools and universities begins to look like some kind of faerie story."

- Graham Hancock

After World War II, Western anthropologists began investigating a strange religion that had developed on numerous archipelagos in the South Pacific. Island populations that had come in contact with technologically advanced cultures (sea-faring Europeans), had developed elaborate religious rituals intended to magically procure the power and wealth of these intruding cultures. This power and wealth was evidenced by the cargo that emerged from the holds of the European ships anchored off-shore.

These island religions became known to western anthropologists as "Cargo Cults." The cargo cult held the belief that if the proper rituals were performed, if the proper rites were observed, shipments of wealth would be delivered to them… from the West… from the "land of the dead." The islanders believed that the cargo in the holds of the European ships was rightfully theirs and had been sent by their ancestors. Such beliefs were consistent with the islander's folklore and mythologies.

"First Contact" with Westerners began in the 1800's. From the perspective of the islanders, arriving trading ships seemed to verify ancient tribal legends. These legends spoke of distant ancestor-gods who had journeyed to the West. Island prophecy held that they would someday return. The West was thought to be the land of the dead... the land of their ancestors.

When trading ships first sailed into the South Pacific, they came from the west... and the strangers aboard were pale skinned... just as the islanders would expect of emissaries coming from the land of the dead. The pre-existing indigenous tradition of the inter-tribal exchange of objects of wealth was integral to the evolving belief that the ancestors and deities were responsible for the arrival of cargo ships. Thus were the ancient legends of the land of the dead verified and fulfilled.

The wide-spread popularity of the South Pacific cargo cults peaked after World War II when the military presence of Japan and the United States faded. By this time, airplanes replaced ships as the vehicles of cargo delivery. Island populations, who had experienced the massive influx of (apparent) technologically advanced cultures and their associated cargo during the war, sought ritualistic means to re-establish the flow of cargo that disappeared with military withdrawal. The Cargo Cult practitioners built replicas of airplanes and landing strips, even radio equipment... imitating sounds associated with airplanes... in their attempt to re-activate the shipments of cargo.

The cargo cult phenomenon, as a religious practice, has appeared in many traditional pre-industrial tribal societies in the wake of interaction with (so-called) technologically advanced cultures. Although not as well documented, similar behaviors have appeared elsewhere in the world... elsewhere in the distant past.

Human history of empirical expansion tells us that when one culture is significantly more technically advanced than the other, the more technologically advantaged culture will be favored by the inevitable disruptive nature of first contact, often with dire consequences for the less technologically advanced society. And so it goes...

Ancient Astronaut Theory

Just as with the archipelagos of the South Pacific, speculative alt-history theorists such as Erich von Däniken… and as popularized by such sensational cable television programming as the History Channel's: *Ancient Aliens*, …have proposed that highly advanced extraterrestrial beings have visited Earth in its antiquity and made "first contact" with our distant ancestors. Such visitors have been popularly labeled "Ancient Astronauts." Proponents suggest that this contact influenced the development of human cultures, technologies and religions. Central to this theory is the assertion that the myriad deities from most (if not all) religions actually were extra-terrestrial entities and that their advanced technologies were interpreted as evidence of their divinity.

According to Ancient Astronaut Theory (AAT), the apparently miraculous achievements of antiquity, such as the construction of the great pyramids in Egypt and Central America, the Moai stone heads of Easter Island and the Nazca lines of Peru… are each remnant examples of this ancient intervention. Per this theory, all prehistoric knowledge, religion, and culture either came directly from extraterrestrial visitors, or were developed as a result of the influence of a cultural incubator or "mother culture" of extra-terrestrial origin.

In regard to scientific rigor, Ancient Astronaut theorists rely primarily on circumstantial evidence of ancient art, craftwork and legend, which they interpret as depicting extraterrestrial technologies and/or contact. Certain curious artifacts of prehistory have been identified as part of the body of evidence in support of AAT… such as the "Saqqara Bird" excavated in the Pa-di-Imen tomb, in Egypt in 1898. This bird-shaped artifact has been carbon-dated to 200 BCE and is speculated to demonstrate that the ancient Egyptians possessed knowledge of advanced aviation principles.

Artifacts from the Americas are also popularly sited by proponents of AAT as having been inspired by extra-terrestrial contact. Multiple Pre Columbian Inca artifacts that were unearthed in excavations in Central and South America look surprisingly similar to modern space shuttles. These tiny gold-carved amulets are estimated to belong to a period between 500 and 800 CE… well over 1000 years old. Traditional archaeologists initially assumed these figurines to be "zoomorphic" or animal shaped talismans.

These artifacts are compelling in that they spark imaginative speculation as to the purpose or intent of those who created them over a millennium ago. As compelling as these objects are… it is the legends and mythologies of the ancients that provide true insight into their world view. Much of the AAT evidence focuses on descriptions of interaction with "the Gods" as told through key passages of early religious texts. Ancient creation myths of gods descending from the heavens… interacting or even interbreeding with early humans, reveals intriguing aspects of how early humans viewed themselves, their world and their place in the grand scheme of the cosmos.

Ancient Mythologies

The 5th Century BCE Sanskrit text, the *Ramayana,* is one of two great *itihāsa,* or historic narrative/teaching epics from India and Nepal. Throughout this epic, the gods routinely travel in transport craft called *Vimanas.* It is not much of an intellectual stretch to compare these "flying cars" or "chariots of the gods" with modern depictions of aircraft, spacecraft or UFOs. Consider this passage from the Ramayana:

"The Pushpaka (flowery vimana) chariot that resembles the Sun and belongs to my brother was brought by the powerful Ravana; that aerial and excellent chariot going everywhere at will… that chariot resembling a bright cloud in the sky… and the King (Rama) got in, and the excellent chariot at the command of the Raghira, rose up into the higher atmosphere."

Such verbiage, from a modern perspective, certainly seems to describe advanced aircraft, if not spacecraft. What is intriguing however, is the etymology of the word: vimana. In addition to meaning a flying chariot, vimana also refers to… (a) God's flying palace… (b) the palace of the supreme monarch… (c) a pyramid shaped temple. And finally, vimana refers to… the science of correct or proportionate measurement of remedies and medicines.

The meaning of the word vimana is perhaps the earliest example of the association of a flying craft (God's flying palace) …with megalithic pyramids (pyramid shaped temple). Flying saucers and pyramids are certainly coincidentally recurring themes in modern AAT. The original Sanskrit: vi-māna literally translates to: traversing or having been measured out. Chariots of the gods... abode of the gods... ancient medicinal metric systems... all could be associated with an extra-ordinary if not divine source or "mother culture."

No discussion of AAT is complete without mentioning the Biblical Old Testament... specifically, the Book of Ezekiel, chapter 1, in which Ezekiel exclaims:

"And I looked, and, behold, a whirlwind came out of the north, a great cloud, and a fire infolding itself, and a brightness was about it, and out of the midst thereof as the colour of amber, out of the midst of the fire."

Ezekiel goes on to describe four winged humanoids, each with four faces (man, lion, ox and eagle) who emerge from a vehicle (or vehicles) that Ezekiel famously describes as wheels within wheels:

"The appearance of the wheels and their work was like unto the colour of a beryl: and they four had one likeness: and their appearance and their work was as it were a wheel in the middle of a wheel."

"As for their rings, they were so high that they were dreadful; and their rings were full of eyes round about them. And when the living creatures went, the wheels went by them: and when the living creatures were lifted up from the earth, the wheels were lifted up."

Particularly interesting is Ezekiel's description of the "rings of eyes" which, if taken as a literal description, conjures up all sorts of imaginative visuals. The Book of Genesis refers to the ancient hybrid "Nephilim" or offspring of the "sons of God" and the "daughters of men" ...which raises the notion of extra-terrestrials having sex with earth women... imaginative visuals indeed.

Abrahamic desert religion mythologies are chuck-full of such lusty imagery... lusty and violent. It was Abraham... the legendary progenitor of Judaism, Christianity and Islam... who, the bible tells us, made "first contact" with other-worldly voices... voices who commanded him to kill his son, Isaac. As Abraham prepares to do the deed... the voices in his head (God, Yahweh or Jehovah) stop him at the last moment, declaring... "Now I know you fear God."

Kill his son, for Christ's sake! No wonder the ancient Gnostics thought that the God Jehovah of the Bible was crazy...

Alien Cargo

There are many more such examples of ancient artifacts, megalithic sites or structures and mythologies that, despite mainstream scientific scrutiny and repudiation, lend themselves quite nicely to circumstantial support of AAT. Taken as a whole, AAT paints an intriguing and somewhat logical narrative concerning the origins of human technology and cosmology. If we hypothetically accept the theory of a global mother culture of extra-terrestrial origin, then all the diverse creation myths around the planet, all the interaction with the gods, take on an eerie commonality. As wildly different as the myths of the various cultures of antiquity are, they could all "fit" within AAT's global premise.

From this perspective... all of Earth's ancient cultures... Sumerian, Egyptian, Incan, Mayan, etc... take on the attributes of a cargo cult. All continents on the planet... China, Africa, the Indian sub-continent, the Americas... have myths and artifacts that could have literally come from the holds of an ancient interstellar spacecraft. Mythic objects like the "Ark of the Covenant" suddenly become ancient alien technology... in the hands of the natives. Within this narrative, precious cargo, contact and interaction with ancient aliens inspired "tales of wonder" in the minds of the locals. Over time, tales became legend, legends became myth... myths were collated and categorized into religions.

The trouble is, this theory is too convenient... to simplistic a solution... to not only humanity's origins, but the very real question of prehistoric extra-terrestrial interaction on Earth. There are other exotic and creative theories that seek to answer the question of the explosion of intelligence and technology that occurred on Earth 10,000 years ago. Theories such as the concept of a prehistoric civilization that had evaded or been forgotten by history. The remnants of such a pre-cataclysmic "ultra-terrestrial" civilization may have provided guidance to a reemerging earthling population, following some pre-diluvian catastrophe.

5
THE ULTRA-TERRESTRIAL

"Right here and now, one quanta away, there is raging a universe of active intelligence that is transhuman, hyperdimensional, and extremely alien... What is driving religious feeling today is a wish for contact with this other universe."

- Terence McKenna

Ancient Astronaut Theory's basic premise is that humanity was "seeded" in its cultural infancy by highly advanced extra-terrestrial beings. This seeding was achieved physically by actual contact and interaction by said beings... physical, flesh and bone beings... that were taken for "Gods" by our ancestors. We have considered circumstantial evidence from around the world in support of this theory, as well as possible responses our ancestors may have had to such contact.

We have examined more recent examples of an isolated culture that had made first contact, with a (supposedly) more highly advanced, interloping culture. The ritualized reaction of Polynesian natives toward the industrialized western world provides insight as to how we might react to extra-terrestrial contact. In considering the Polynesian response, we have the luxury of examining an instance of clashing cultures... both of terrestrial origin. It has not been until the modern era that such a vast disparity in technologies has allowed for such a perspective.

But what if such a great disparity between earthling cultures and technologies did exist in our distant past? What if an even greater technological discrepancy exists today, not between us and some isolated indigenous tribe, but between us and a highly advanced, globally intact yet undetectable earthling culture? A culture so advanced, that it demonstrates science fiction author, Arthur C. Clark's famous third law that states: *Any sufficiently advanced technology is indistinguishable from magic.*

Such is the concept of Ultra-Terrestrial Theory (UTT).

The idea of a pan-global, millennia old, technologically advanced civilization that has for reasons of their own, remained hidden from most, if not all of humanity, seems unlikely at first glance. But in comparison to AAT considered above, UTT would answer or "fit" all of the same criteria concerning humanity's amazing feats of antiquity and mythological similarities. It would also seem to explain specific ancient myths pertaining lost civilizations, such as the Greek philosopher and mathematician, Plato's reference to Atlantis.

It would also solve or eliminate the insurmountable challenges of physical inter-stellar space travel. UFOs of earthly, ultra-terrestrial origin would not have to contend with the unfathomable distances between star systems. In light of UTT, mythological and religious accounts of contact with "The Gods" are still within the realm of logic, albeit slightly weirder. Consider the biblical Nephilim, referenced earlier...

The Nephilim (plural) are (1) the offspring of the "sons of God" and the "daughters of men." or (2) "giants" who inhabit Canaan. Etymology: "Nephilim" (נְפִילִים) probably derives from the Hebrew root npl (נָפַל), "to fall" which also includes: "to cause to fall" and "to kill, to ruin."

The "sons of God" who fathered the hybrid Nephilim, are referred to as "fallen ones" throughout ancient biblical literature. In difference to the connotation that the fallen ones are analogous to "fallen angels" (AKA; the shining one: Lucifer, et al), a more literal interpretation can be considered. Use of the term "the fallen ones" or simply "the fallen" by our ancestors may have actually been referencing a fallen empire or civilization, similar to how we refer to the fall of the Roman Empire today. Additionally, the Book of Enoch connects the Nephilim directly to the "egrēgoroi," translated as "the watchers."

In the ancient Judaic religious text, the *Book of Enoch*, the egrēgoroi are originally assigned to watch over humanity, but become covetous of earth women. They eventually proceed to not only procreate, but illicitly instruct humans, teaching them in arts and technologies such as weaponry, sorcery, and other techniques, thereby greatly accelerating humanity's technological development. In light of this, the watchers can be viewed as part of a "mother culture" of terrestrial origin… representatives or perhaps remnants a pan-global, technologically advanced civilization… possibly even remnants of a distinct, separate humanoid species.

Again, this concept raises similarities to other ancient mythologies such as tales of the lost continent of Atlantis and/or Lemuria. The Lemurian mythos includes a contemporary urban legend from North America, pertaining to a secret base, hidden deep inside Mount Shasta, located in northern California, USA. This mythology is currently alive and well in the rural and "new age" communities adjacent to the mountain. We shall return to the topic of Mount Shasta, shortly.

The mythology of a technologically advanced, remnant group of "watchers," living within snow-clad mountains is repeated around the globe. The Russian occultist, Helena Petrovna Blavatsky, widely known as: Madam Blavatsky, co-founded the 19th century Theosophical Society. The Theosophical Society had their "Masters of the Ancient Wisdom," a highly evolved body of teachers (Mahatmas). Blavatsky's Mahatmas were not considered disembodied beings, but highly evolved earthlings involved in overseeing the spiritual growth of individual humans and the development of civilizations.

Other spiritualist luminaries of the era who incorporated the concept of "ascended masters" in their mythic systems include: Aleister Crowley (Thelema), Alice A. Bailey (New Group of World Servers), Geraldine Innocente (The Bridge to Freedom), Elizabeth Clare Prophet (Church Universal and Triumphant), Benjamin Creme (Share International) and last but not least: Guy Ballard.

In 1930, Ballard was hiking on Mount Shasta… a 14,179 foot, snow-clad (and potentially active) volcano, located at the southern end of the Cascade Range in Siskiyou County, California... when he encountered a being that identified himself as the ascended master, Saint Germain. This encounter resulted in the creation of the "I AM" Activity. The I AM movement is considered an offshoot of theosophy and a major precursor to several New Age religions.

All of the spiritualists listed above share the "adepts residing within high-mountain sanctuaries" motif. The "ascended masters" mythology blurs the boundary between technology and magic... between science and spiritualism. But, given Clark's third law, mentioned above, perhaps the distance between science and spirit are not that great... perhaps there is no boundary.

A highly advanced mother culture civilization, having fallen from its height of power, covertly watching and assisting a more primitive population... technologically answers the questions concerning the rapid development of prehistoric cultures, raised in Ancient Astronaut theory. A spiritually advanced counsel of ascended "Mahatmas" or masters, guiding early humanity, may answer the same questions... from a different perspective. Perhaps a pan-global, millennia old, technologically advanced civilization... as opposed to an ancient world-wide order of illuminated mystic masters... are, in reality, one and the same entity. The perceived differences only reflect the different world views and sophistication of understanding of those who came in contact with the entity. After all... reality is in the eye of the beholder.

Fungus Amongus

The question remains... Was humanity "seeded" in its cultural infancy by a highly advanced and undetectable, co-existing earthling culture? A culture so advanced that it demonstrates Arthur C. Clark's third law? Skeptics consider such theories to be too outlandish... too "tin-foil-hat-ish" to be taken with any measure of seriousness. However, the theories examined above may, in fact, be too mundane... too comfortable in their vision.

Like the classic science fiction tales of Clark, Bradbury, et al, the anthropomorphic explanations presented by ATT enthusiasts, conveniently feature human or bi-pedal humanoid extra-terrestrials that look just like us. These theories fit quite nicely in our earth-centric, hominid view of universe. The true origins of extra-terrestrial intelligence on earth may be far stranger... far more unfathomable and fantastic than some metal hulled ship... careening through space... carrying humanoid visitors to our planet.

It is likely that life in universe is far more plentiful, diverse and truly "alien" than our imaginations are normally willing to wrap around. Entities that bear little resemblance to life as we define it on earth (let alone bipedal humans) may fill the cosmos. One fascinating hypothesis suggests that the void of space, conventionally considered lifeless, is teaming with life. The term used to describe this theorized life-form is... "extra-terrestrial extremophile."

An extremophile is defined as an organism that thrives in physically or geochemically extreme conditions... in this example, the absence of a gravity-bound atmosphere. "Research has proven that extreme organisms can live in very harsh environments. Such extremophiles can survive almost everywhere, including in outer space" ...says neuropsychologist, Dr. Rhawn Joseph.

Dr. Joseph has investigated NASA footage that shows what he believes to be living alien organisms in the vicinity of the space shuttle Columbia, during NASA's so-called "broken tether" incident, in 1996. According to Dr. Joseph, many of these objects are huge in size and have a pulsating nucleus, which could be an indication that they are living life-forms. These objects are alleged to be able to suddenly change direction and speed of movement.

Reportedly, thousands of these creatures observed by NASA appear to be exceedingly similar to a species of algae known as *eudorina elegans*, but had to be many kilometers in size. In other words, there are millions of strange objects in space which could be living extraterrestrial organisms. Astronauts could see these objects outside the space shuttle, travelling along-side the shuttle and have described some of these objects as "definitely not solid", "plasma-like" and tissue paper thin, and engaging in unusual movements.

The implication here is that biological life may exist throughout the vastness of space. Biological life may traverse not only within solar systems, but between the stars... possibly between galaxies. Terrestrial life may be seeded by these life-forms getting caught in the gravity well of a planetary system and metamorphosing into a terrestrial-based life-form. Perhaps parasitic forms of life "catch a ride" on these entities, thereby increasing the possibility of inter-stellar migration of biological life...

The Magic Mushroom

Still, the question of the inter-stellar seeding of "intelligent" life remains. Are there any known species of extremophile that could survive in the vacuum of space? If so, how would such an example escape a planetary atmosphere? Moreover, are there earthly examples of an extremophile that interacts or effects human intelligence? These questions lead us to a psychedelic variation on the biological inter-stellar migration theory. The life classification of interest comes from the fungi kingdom (taxonomic rank).

A fungus is a member of a large group of eukaryotic organisms that includes micro-organisms such as yeasts and molds, as well as our species class of interest, the noble mushroom. The name "mushroom" typically refers to those fungi that have a stem, a cap and gills (or pores) on the underside of the cap. The mushroom reproduces via the dispersal of microscopic spores, capable of surviving for extended periods of time in extremely unfavorable conditions. The following is an excerpt from American lecturer, and author: Terrence McKenna, on the subject of extra-terrestrial life:

My candidate for that kind of an intrusive extra-terrestrial would probably be a mushroom of some sort, or a spore-bearing life form, because spores are very impervious to low temperatures and high radiation... the kind of environment met with in outer space. There's no question that through what's called Brownian motion, which is sort of random percolation, spores do reach the outer edge of our atmosphere, and there, in the presence of cosmic rays and meteors and rare, highly energetic events, occasionally a very small percentage of these biological objects are wafted into space. We even possess meteorites that are believed to be pieces of the Martian surface, thrown out by impacts on the Martian surface of asteroidal material.

In fact I think part of the grappling with the (extra-terrestrial) mystery is going to lead to the conclusion that space is not an impermeable and insurmountable barrier to biology... that in fact planets are islands, and life does occasionally wash in from distant places, and if conditions are correct, can take hold. However, let me say we are dealing, not simply with the phenomenon of extraterrestrial biology, but with the phenomenon of extra-terrestrial intelligence, and this is a hackle-raising notion."

-Terrence McKenna

Certain species of mushroom commonly referred to as "Magic Mushrooms" when ingested, have a psychedelic effect on the nervous system of humans. This effect is characterized by hallucinogenic perception, often revelatory and insightful in nature. This psychedelic experience is so profound, it is often considered to be a form of communication between the ingested mushroom and the human host. Communication infers intelligent interaction between two sentient entities.

Let us explore the "novel" concept of human interaction with an intelligent spore-bearing life form, what we will call the Magic Mushroom Theory, in greater detail...

The crux of the Magic Mushroom Theory is that the psychoactive effect of specific mushrooms on the human nervous system constitutes a form of communication between species. It presumes that communication denotes intelligence, and is a form of cognizance and consciousness. This intelligence is in a state of suspended animation during the mushroom's spore phase. It becomes potentially highly active and accessible, via ingestion by a human, during the mushroom's growth and maturity phase.

Here is the mythology...

An alien mushroom spore in a state of suspended animation, drifting in space, is caught in Earth's atmosphere. It floats to the surface of the planet, where, under the right conditions, it germinates (possibly mutates) and grows into a mushroom. An unsuspecting earthling hominid finds and eats the mushroom. As it is digested, the mushroom's reanimated psycho-active properties course through the earthling's bloodstream, ultimately reaching the brain. As the psycho-active properties take effect... "Contact."

This is a symbiotic relationship. The alien symbiont... or mushroom... requires an interface with a biological nervous system, in order to access and activate its consciousness. It also requires a nervous system's perceptive and motor function capabilities in order to perceive and manipulate its new, three dimensional environment. In other words, the mushroom needs a body to move around in, a brain to "think" in, and eyes with which to see. Once it enters into a symbiotic relationship with our earthling, it is free to interact and explore in this strange new world, by co-operating or sharing the host's body.

In return, upon entering into symbiosis via ingestion, the earthling host gains access to the mushroom's molecular data-base. The intelligence that has been in a compressed stasis (i.e. "biological" bit-rate reduction) within the spore, decompresses during the growth cycle of the mushroom and becomes readable upon interface with the host's nervous system. Both entities now have access to this data. The information that is transmitted to the earthling takes the form of revelation and insight… thereby increasing the earthling's knowledge base and subsequent intelligence.

In this simplistic example, the alien intelligence that is the mushroom makes contact with humanoid earthlings in a mutually advantageous, win-win, close encounter. No spacecraft necessary. Mushroom spores from outer space are, de facto, extra-terrestrial. For purposes of taking our "Magic Mushroom Theory" to its extreme: humanity's discovery and ingestion of the magic fruit of the spore is the close encounter… contact… with alien life. Accordingly, humanity's explosion of intelligence may very well have been driven by the revelatory and insightful nature of the effect that magic mushrooms have on the human nervous system.

Regardless of the above, there is no doubt that fungi are a (forgive the pun) trippy life-form. A giant *Armillaria Solidipes* fungus, a species of honey mushroom in the Malheur National Forest in Oregon, was found to span 8.9 km (2,200 acres), which would make it the largest organism on earth, by area. Talk about a space colony.

While the notion of an extra-terrestrial spore-bearing life form literally seeding planet Earth with an intelligence agent from distant star systems, is certainly fascinating… the same scenario from an Ultra-Terrestrial standpoint, is perhaps more intriguing. If an anciently occurring psychedelic variety of fungi species, as they have evolved on Earth, are themselves considered to be an Ultra-Terrestrial intelligence… then theories of ancient intervention begin to get seriously interesting.

In this scenario, the mushroom, as ultra-terrestrial, allegorically becomes, for example… the highly evolved teacher or body of teachers or Mahatmas of Blavatsky fame. The psychedelic revelations of the ingested mushroom, becomes the sacred teachings. In other words, the mushroom becomes the Mahatma. Much more on this later.

Mushroom Cult

Human history is full of cosmologies with "deified" mushrooms included in their iconography. The oldest artistic representations of hallucinogenic mushrooms in the world are found in the Tassilli Mountains in the Sahara Dessert. These rock paintings, created by pre-neolithic hunters and gatherers are between 7,000 and 9,000 years old. They might be the most ancient human culture as yet documented in which the ritual use of hallucinogenic mushrooms is explicitly represented. It is fitting that Africa, considered by many to be the cradle of humanity, is also home to the oldest known mushroom cult.

Some scholars believe that the deified plant "soma" mentioned in the ancient Hindu text, the Rigveda, was in fact the psychoactive mushroom: *Amanita Muscaria*. Out of the ten Rigveda books, the ninth hymn book, *Soma Mandala*, is devoted entirely to Soma. The Vedas state that the god-plant Soma was found in the mountains and that the intoxicating juices from Soma were expressed from the flesh of the plant using so-called "Soma-stones." In the text it is stated that drinking soma produces immortality...

"We have drunk Soma and become immortal; we have attained the light the Gods discovered."
- Rigveda (8.43.3)

The Sanskrit word for immortality is Amrita. Amrita is phonetically and conceptually very similar to the Greek ambrosia; both are what the gods drink ...and what made them deities. Ancient Greece was home to a ritual cult that lasted for 2,000 years until it was suppressed by Christianity. This cult, known as the Eleusinian Mysteries, consisted of secret teachings conferred by high adepts, to a body of initiates who, once a year in September or early October, came to the Eleusian plains for worship of the Gods. The mysteries took two forms... the lesser and greater mysteries.

The greater mysteries took place in the fall. These greater rites were preformed with the ingestion of a substance called kykeon, variously described as being made from barley and pennyroyal and/or from rye ergot (from which LSD-25 was synthesized). As such, it has been proposed by some scholars that this Mystery cult was associated with some manner of hallucinogen. In this speculation, it is worth noting that September through October is the season of the mushroom, in Europe.

In the Old Testament, there are many references to a spiritual food sent down from heaven by God, called manna. The Bible's first reference to manna is in the Book of Exodus, as the children of Israel are fleeing from Egypt. After many weeks of wandering, they began complaining to Moses, their religious leader and lawgiver, that they are tired and hungry. It is at this point in the Biblical narrative when God intervenes...

"Then said the LORD unto Moses, Behold, I will rain bread from heaven for you; and the people shall go out and gather a certain rate every day, that I may prove them, whether they will walk in my law or no (16:4). And when the dew that lay was gone up, behold, upon the face of the wilderness there lay a small round thing, as small as the hoar frost on the ground (16: 14). And when the children of Israel saw it, they said one to another It is manna: for they wist not what it was. And Moses said unto them, this is the bread which the Lord hath given you to eat."

In his notorious book: *The Sacred Mushroom and the Cross: A Study of the Nature and Origins of Christianity Within the Fertility Cults of the Ancient Near East,* published in 1970, English archaeologist and Dead Sea Scrolls scholar, John Marco Allegro presented a theory that shook the world of scholars studying the early Christian era. In his book, Allegro compared the development of language to the development of myths, religions, and cultic practices in world cultures... specifically, the linguistics of early Christianity and fertility cults in the Ancient Near East.

In that work, Allegro argued that the renowned biblical Rabbi known to us as "Jesus" never existed and was a mythological creation of early Christians under the influence of psychoactive mushroom extracts such as psilocybin. He maintained that the roots of Christianity, as of many other religions, lay in fertility cults, and that cult practices, such as the ritual ingestion of Amanita Muscaria, was in fact the early church's Eucharist.

Upon its publication, Allegro's work was ridiculed by his peers. Biblical scholars in Britain went so far as to suggest that the new book looked like the "psychedelic ravings of a hippie cultist." Recent studies of Allegro's work however, have given new supporting linguistic evidence and led to calls for his theories to be re-evaluated by mainstream academia.

Historical use of the Psilocybin mushroom has strong evidence in Central America. Mushroom use was prevalent in Mexico prior the Spanish conquest and an important aspect of Mexican religion and life. The fungi were sacred and used in divination and healing. Mushroom stones have been unearthed from as far back as 1000 B.C.E. The mushroom using peoples of the Americas held on to their traditions from antiquity and through the violent persecution of the Spanish, until it was (coincidently?) rediscovered in the early 1950's.

"When we look at the mushroom stones we must always remember that in pre-Conquest times most art, if not all, was religious, as it once was in Europe. And we must remember that the hold on the inner life of the Mesoamerican peoples of the ethnogeny, notably the entheogenic mushrooms, was all-powerful, as it is to this day in remote corners of highland Mexico. Those who have not explored the role of the entheogens in the cultural past of Mesoamerica easily overlook that role or assume that it was of minor importance, solely because for us it is of no importance."

— R Gordon Wasson

The myriad of mushroom cults throughout history and from around the world, make a compelling case for the integral role that psychoactive substances played in humanity's remarkable intellectual development over the last 10,000 years. Again, the ingestion of the *psilocybin cubensis* mushroom, as an agent of human evolution, was strongly argued by Terence McKenna in his book: *Food of the Gods* (1992). He theorized that the consumption of these mushrooms, as a component of early man's daily diet, triggered the expansion of human consciousness. This expansion was directly responsible for the intellectual and cultural development of modern man.

The mushroom, according to McKenna, had also given early humans their first truly religious experiences, which were the basis for the foundation of all subsequent earthling religions. Given the above, the globally present mushroom cult in all probability co-evolved with humanity over the last 10,000 years… the era of man. As an agent of change, the magic mushroom and its human host's organizational structure, or cult, that developed around it, was instrumental in humanity's strategic thinking and tool building.

Perhaps the mushroom cults that have existed around the world, for the last 10,000 years, are the ultimate Cargo Cult. In the context of the Magic Mushroom Theory, the cargo was not delivered by any sea faring or space faring vessel, but was delivered to earth in the form of a tiny spore. This delivery was not initiated by exploration… rather it was delivered by migration. A migration of microscopic mushroom spores… drifting through space… across the unimaginable distances between stars… over unimaginable periods of time. Just as the coconut washes ashore upon a South Pacific archipelago, so does the extra-terrestrial agent of change wash ashore upon spaceship earth, carrying within its tiny spore, the precious cargo of intelligence.

With McKenna's "Food of the Gods" theory, we begin to see that the seemingly divergent theories presented herein, begin to fall into place. The magic mushroom either becomes an evolutionary ultra-terrestrial "agent of intelligence" for humanity, or it additionally becomes an extra-terrestrial intelligence catalyst, depending on how far one wants to take the theory.

Indeed, the magic mushroom theory takes on new synchronistic significance at the close of the Second World War. Converging events seem to conspire in the following decades that give new meaning to the concept of mushroom cult. Although it is not common knowledge yet, 1940's era scientists at Sandoz Pharmaceuticals have synthesized the next psychedelic trigger.

The psychedelic revolution of the sixties was ignited, in part, by the Magic Mushroom, as re-discovered by operatives of the Central Intelligence Agency. As we shall see, another incredible coincidence is unfolding with the discovery of LSD-25, the widespread use of which was also facilitated by the CIA. Interestingly, the CIA itself emerged out of the post World War II era… being created in 1947 by President Harry S Truman.

In the next chapter, we will consider the events of post WWII, in light of the strange psychedelic theories presented herein. Psychedelics as an intelligence agent, puts an ironic twist to the nefarious exploits and intentions of the CIA. That lesson in irony being… "Be careful what you wish for, for it will surely come true." We will see how the old paradigm ended, and the brave new world came to be. We will consider how the old "Age of Pisces" came crashing to a close, while the new "Age of Aquarius" sprang forth. Additionally, we will scrutinize what part the outlaw chemical of consciousness, LSD-25, played in this epochal transformation.

6
PSYCHEDELIC APOCALYPSE

"I sat in the dark and thought: There's no big apocalypse... just an endless procession of little ones."

- Neil Gaiman

It is only now; half a century after it all began... now that the cosmic roller-coaster that was the "Psychedelic Sixties" has come to a complete stop... only now that the story can be told. After years of processing and perspective... after the assassination of John and Robert Kennedy... of Dr Martin Luther King and Malcolm X... after the death of John Lennon, Robert Marley and Jerry Garcia... after the death of the very Ken Kesey and Dr Timothy Leary... that the story... the epic tale... the new mythology... can be fully told.

They say time heals all wounds. After the era that has come to be known simply as "the sixties" is but a distant memory... after disco and punk and cyberpunk... after Apple Corp[13] and Apple Computer[14] ...after the contemporary computer-compiled-collective-consciousness has been embraced and the world made new again... can the enormity of what transpired... be appreciated. Yes... time

---

[13] Apple Corps Ltd (aka: Apple) is a multimedia corporation founded in London in January 1968 by the members of the Beatles, which replaced their earlier company, Beatles Ltd.

[14] Apple Inc., formerly Apple Computer, Inc., is an American multinational corporation headquartered in Cupertino, California.

was the necessary ingredient... time to reflect upon the neon sun-set that was the millennium and to contemplate the gathering darkness that obscures... yet is... our near future.

What follows is a retrospective understanding of not only the importance of the psychedelic sixties as a cultural well-spring, but as a powerful catalyst of transition into the new paradigm that is, depending upon perspective, either the "new age" or the "new world order."

The Yankee and Cowboy War

Since before its founding in 1776, the history of America's colonization and expansion is one of embattled ideologies, competing for dominance and control of the American socio-political landscape. Indeed, what was to become the United States of America was born of violent revolution against the British Empire. New world colonists, dissatisfied over taxation without representation, staged the (original) Tea Party to protest colonial tyranny... thereby sparking the first American Revolution.

The very essence of what has been called the American Experience was founded upon contentious ideology. Other illustrations of colliding American ideologies include: Settlers (European invaders) vs. Native Tribes (indigenous population), North (yankee) vs. South (rebel), Democrat (jackass) vs. Republican (elephant), etc. A contemporary, albeit slightly more obscure example of such dichotomy is what can be referred to as the clash between the Eastern Yankee and the Western Cowboy.

In 1976, Carl Oglesby published a book entitled: *The Yankee and Cowboy War: Conspiracies from Dallas to Watergate.* In that book, Oglesby outlines one version of the concept that there exists in the United States, a power struggle between the East Coast, Ivy League, powers-that-be, Yankee establishment, pedigreed old money... and the West Coast, Nuevo riche, big oil, silicon valley, Cowboy upstart new money. Oglesby argued that the seemingly unrelated events of Dallas (JFK assassination, 1963), Memphis (MLK assassination, 1968), Watergate (DNC break-in, 1972)... even the demise of the Howard Hughes empire... were all tied together in a vast conspiracy whereby one power elite attempts to overthrow and replace the other.

These monumental events of US history, viewed from the

perspective of the Yankee and Cowboy war, take on new and interesting nuances concerning "who is really pulling the strings" in American politics of power. Seemingly unrelated events "fall into place" in light of the possibility of an East Coast verses West Coast power elite struggle. As in all good conspiracies, there potentially exist multiple factions... indeed factions within factions... in each power elite camp. Possible factions include... the mob, the CIA, organized labor, Goldman Sachs, the high tech industry, the Heritage Foundation, the Hollywood establishment, NASA, the Supreme Court... the list goes on & on (don't even get me started on the Trilateral Commission, Bilderbegers, etc).

The question becomes... which faction is battling for which power elite? Are they loyal? ...and under what circumstances do they switch sides? For instance, what clandestine role does NASA play in its off-world operations and is NASA Yankee controlled... or does it align with Cowboy high tech? What exactly is the "California Ideology" and is it neoliberal, neoconservative or both? ...or neither?

Oh what a tangled web.

There is enough fodder in Oglesby's Yankee-Cowboy power elite premise to keep any respectable conspiracy theorist busy for many a computer screen lit... Red Bull fuelled... search-engine driven night of research and hypothesizing. Contemporary parapolitical issues especially post 9/11, take on an even more sinister shade, given Oglesby's theory.

What "black ops" organizations were put into play in the name of Homeland Security... devoid of any congressional oversight... in the days and weeks that followed 9/11? The ramifications of the afore mentioned *Top Secret America* suggest a splintering of motivations of these cabals, rather than a unified America standing up to international terrorism. As a result, the puzzle pieces that are contemporary American politics suddenly re-arrange in interesting and sinister ways.

Contemporary election cycles alone are mind-bending within the Yankee-Cowboy war hypothesis. On which side do current national political figures fall, in this scenario? The recent rise of self-funded billionaire candidates in American politics, speaks volumes. In light of the above, the curious are encouraged to dig deeper into this theory. Yet our interest is focused upon another, more arcane facet of the Yankee-Cowboy power struggle.

This author suggests that during the exact same timeline as Oglesby's East-West discord, there existed a co-occurring and deeper struggle, waged for the very soul of America... especially the American youth. This was a deeper struggle in the sense that its influence went beyond political, into the cultural and psychological... indeed the archetypical framework of American consciousness. Lines were being drawn as to whether the corporate overlord consumer culture was to remain the dominant paradigm, or was a spiritual and cultural revolution underway?

The Yankee and Cowboy Psychedelic War

Amid the socio-political turmoil of the era, immediately following World War II, there was in America a lotus-blossoming of philosophical and spiritual inner exploration. This was fueled in part by the increasing interest and availability to the Western World, of materials on comparative religions of the East, especially those of Buddhism and Hinduism. Interest in Theosophy from the previous century, along with the works of Herman Hesse, Aldus Huxley and Alan Watts added fuel to the fire of what was to become the new Western spiritual quest.

If Eastern spiritualism acted as fuel to a newly kindled philosophic fire, psychoactive substances, most notably LSD-25, acted like gasoline thrown onto the figurative flame.

LSD-25... that hideous/wondrous trickster... that two-faced creator/destroyer Shiva, sipping soma from an ornate goblet, carved from a human skull... pearlescent jewel of day-glow night-light... neon-petaled unfolding radiant vision... perfectly (both literally and metaphorically) encapsulated for the West in the form of a little pill. Enlightenment in a bottle... conveniently manufactured for the West by the neo-alchemists at Sandoz laboratories.

Just prior to WWII, the Swiss chemical manufacturer, Sandoz Pharmaceuticals, seeking to expand its market, began to research various drug compounds. The initial goal of Sandoz research was to develop a possible circulatory and respiratory stimulant. A promising young Swiss research chemist at Sandoz, Dr Albert Hoffman, had been methodically synthesizing variations of the Ergot fungus:

Claviceps purpurea.

On Friday, April 16, 1943 a curious premonition overtook Dr Hoffman, causing him to "take another look" at the 25th compound of the lysergic acid series, labeled: LSD-25... a curious, synchronistic and profoundly fateful premonition. Indeed the future course of Western spirituality hung in the balance... pivoted on Hoffman's curiosity. The result of his re-investigation was the now infamous bike ride through the streets of Basle. Hoffman had inadvertently, most likely through absorption of the skin, taken the world's first "acid trip."

Subsequent experimentation revealed that miniscule amounts, 200 millionths of one gram, produced phenomenal effects, including vivid hallucinations. This made LSD-25, the most powerful psychoactive chemical known to man... a veritable psychedelic genie in a bottle.

In the decades following World War II, LSD-25 was to find its way to both coasts of North America... facilitated, strangely enough, by non-other than the Central Intelligence Agency. It is unclear what nefarious end, beyond mind control, that the CIA sought... some contend that they sought the militarization of the mind. Little did the spooks at the CIA know, they were about to set loose a counter-cultural revolution... an archaic revival... the likes of which hadn't been seen since the Festival at Eleusis.

Mirroring the dichotomy of the Eastern and Western philosophical tradition... born of it... was the distinctly American manifestation of what was to become an emergent psychedelic cultural revolution. The term "psychedelic" is derived from the Greek words psihi and diloun... which translates to... "soul manifesting." The following from Wikipedia, succinctly defines the psychedelic experience...

...A psychedelic experience is characterized by the striking perception of aspects of one's mind previously unknown, or by the creative exuberance of the mind liberated from its ostensibly ordinary fetters.

The American East Coast approached psychedelia in a distinctly different manner than did the American West. Yankees and Cowboys... Each coast had its unique spin on the burgeoning psychedelic culture, complete with holy places, heroes and villains...

The East Coast lineup included such lysergic luminaries as Drs Timothy Leary, Richard Alpert and Ralph Metzner. Known as the "Cambridge Three" ...all three were professors at the pride of the Ivy League: Harvard University. While at Harvard, beginning in 1960, the good doctors conducted research on the effects of psychoactive substances. This study was known as the Harvard Psilocybin Project.[15]

In 1964, Leary, Alpert and Metzner would co-author and publish: *The Psychedelic Experience: A Manual Based on the Tibetan Book of the Dead*. This collaborative work was intended to be an instruction manual for guiding participants and facilitators during psychedelic drug sessions or "trips." Also known as the *Bardo Thodol*, the *Tibetan Book of the Dead* is an ancient Buddhist manual on death and dying. It guides one through the stages of death and subsequent rebirth. In addition to Leary, et al, this curious Buddhist text would prove to have a profound and synchronistic influence on one of the greatest minds of modern psychology.

Leary and Alpert went beyond academia... to embrace, each in their own way, pop-culture and the media of the era. Leaving Harvard... each went on to establish his own intertwining psychedelic sub-faction. Adopting the vernacular and attire of the times, Leary & Alpert's love beads and stylish "Nehru" jackets, made them the "darlings" of the press. They also colonized the holy psychedelic sanctuary of the sixties, a rambling old mansion in up-state New York, infamously known as "Millbrook," thereby defining the East-coast intellectual Yankee psychedelic scene.

In the ensuing years, Leary would embrace the "Western" path, which included the flower-power hippie scene of the era. He would go on to advocate emerging technological aspects of the western world, such as the early transhumanism movement, the colonization of space via his SMI^{2}LE[16] material and the soon-to appear personal computing revolution. Leary was a prolific author, writing such titles as *The Politics of Ecstasy* (1968), *StarSeed* (1973) and *Chaos and Cyber Culture* (1994).

Alpert would embrace the "Eastern" path of enlightenment, traveling to India in 1967, where he met his Guru, Maharaj-ji and ultimately adopting the Hindi name "Ram Dass." Ram Dass would go on to become a much loved American spiritual teacher. He is

---

[15] See: https://en.wikipedia.org/wiki/Harvard_Psilocybin_Project
[16] Acronym for: Space Migration, Intellegence Increase & Life Extension

perhaps best known for authoring the now-classic book on spirituality, yoga and meditation: *Be Here Now* (1971).

The West Coast psychonauts consisted, in part, of Oregon Author Ken Kesey, the Merry Pranksters and poet & lyricist Robert Hunter, of Grateful Dead fame. Kesey, the pranksters & Hunter all epitomized the San Francisco flower power scene of the era, representing the heirs apparent of the SF "Beat" scene. Kesey & Hunter were both indoctrinated into psychedelia by volunteering as research subjects for the CIA backed experiments involving LSD-25 and other psychedelic drugs.

Project MK-ULTRA[17] was the code name of a covert U.S. government human research operation, that experimented in various methods of behavioral engineering of humans (read: mind control) through the CIA's Scientific Intelligence Division. This covert (and highly illegal) experimentation commenced in 1959 at the Menlo Park Veterans Hospital and continued into the late 1960s at Kesey's alma mater, the West Coast's pillar of learning: Stanford University.

Kesey would parley his writing talent, along with his experiences/visions from the MK-ULTRA experimentations to pen, not one but two great novels... *One Flew over the Cookoo's Nest* (1962) and *Sometimes a Great Notion* (1964). Interestingly, Kesey subsequently sold the movie rights to *Cookoo's Nest* to actor Kurt Douglas for $10,000, (a deal signed on that time-honored legal document: the bar napkin) and used the money to buy a dilapidated old school bus he named "Further." Famous in its own right, *Further* became the transport vehicle for Kesey's early psychedelic experimentation with the multi-media-mind theater extravaganzas that came to be known as "Acid Tests."

The name "Acid Test" was adopted by Kesey, taken from the term "acid test" used by gold miners in the 1850s. This metallurgical (and Alchemical sounding) test used a strong acid to distinguish gold from base metals.

For its time, this was cutting edge pop-culture at its weirdest. The Acid Tests were initially house parties at Kesey's La Honda, CA home, where LSD-25 was freely dispersed as a psychedelic "party favor." These parties soon expanded into larger public venues, such as San Francisco's Fillmore Auditorium. Soon psychedelic posters

---

[17] See: http://www.princeton.edu/~achaney/tmve/wiki100k/docs/ Project_MKULTRA.html

appeared up and down the West Coast asking… "Can You Pass the Acid Test?" Kesey's Acid Tests became the travelling psychedelic circus/tabernacle that defined the West-coast-hippy Cowboy psychedelic scene.

The Kesey/Hunter connection deepened as Hunter became the lyricist for the Grateful Dead, the "House Band" of Kesey's Acid Tests. Often overlooked in retrospectives on the sixties, Hunter's skill as a poet and lyricist proved to be profound in shaping the psychedelic sixties. His collaboration with the Grateful Dead's lead guitarist, Jerry Garcia (1942 to 1995) resulted in some of the most iconic, psychedelic musical compositions of the era.

In regard to scientific research, both Harvard and Stanford appear to have been independently researching psychedelia at approximately the same time… and (coincidentally?) some of the same political factions identified in Oglesby's book, are also nefariously at work behind the scenes of the fledgling psychedelic revolution. As the so-called "cold war" was at its coldest during this time, interest in psychedelics by these various factions goes beyond coincidence.

Thus began the Yankee and Cowboy Psychedelic War… a campaign of consciousness… a war fought on two fronts, East and West… pitting two distinct counter-cultural movements, as the manifested on each coast, against "The Man" the establishment… the military-industrial complex… the status quo. The Yankee and Cowboy psychedelic war became a psychic struggle, waged between the powers of conformity and consciousness. Each coast's psychedelic faction brought their philosophic tactics designed to "break on through" the doors of perception. Needless to say, this scared the hell out of the powers of conformity.

Again, the dichotomy between the East and West coasts, produced factions of ideals… cabals of competing psychedelic strategies… in the war against the establishment. Tellingly, the origin of the word "War" is from the Old High German: *werran,* meaning to confuse… for the sixties were necessarily confusing times in America. The innocence of the Eisenhower years were slipping away, even as the military-industrial complex Ike warned us about… was cranking up.

In retrospect, the sixties appear to be a high-water mark for America. The sixties were the apex, the zenith of American culture. What has euphemistically been called "American Exceptionalism," peaked by the summer of 1967. The sixties foreshadowed the true beginning of the new millennium... the brave new world. It also marked the long downhill slide of the American experience, arguably facilitated by the Military-Industrial Complex... more on this in our next chapter.

From the perspective of hindsight, the sixties counterculture was the first reaction, the first response to the industrial-military complex... the machine... or in Kesey's words... *the combine*. The sixties counterculture would become the "first strike against the Empire." The effects of this psychedelic revolution... this psychic war... are still being played out today. The so-called counterculture of the sixties was the earliest beginning... the precursor, if you will... to the social networking of the 21st century.

As we have since seen, change of this magnitude takes time. Time is an integral and necessary ingredient of our cultural awakening. Like progress, cultural awakening does not always proceed in a straight line. Two steps forward, one step back. Even after more than fifty years... not all facets are known. Indeed, even today, not all factors put into play in '67 have come into full fruition. Not all the cards are on the table... a few hands from this game have yet to be played.

What began with Leary, et al on the East coast and Kesey & company in the West, is much more important than we realize... even today. The seed of psychedlia that was then planted, has germinated... incubated... and quietly blossomed... lotus-like... into a new world view, beyond McLuhan's global village... to a global mind. The psychedelic experience revealed, to a large cross-section of American youth, dimensions of the mind only hinted at in philosophic and spiritual texts.

In the west, the Summer of Love mutated... migrated to the South Bay, where it would rest dormant for a decade, in an area of Northern California that would soon launch the next phase of American innovation and entrepreneurship, a strange brew of fiscal conservatism and "dotcom" neoliberalism, some have called the *California Ideology*. This sleepy region, just south of San Francisco, now recognized as the birthplace of the computer revolution, would soon become known, world-wide as: Silicon Valley.

The rise and proliferation of personal computing... as a technology of personal freedom... is a now-obvious outcome of the incubator that was the sixties. What occurred then is inextricably tied to who we are now and who we will become. For the psychedelic experience, drugs aside, is the consciousness of the future… and in the words of Kesey… *"You're either on the Bus, or you're off the Bus."*

7
WELCOME TO THE SPOOK SHOW

"In a very real and terrifying sense, our Government is the CIA and the Pentagon... with Congress reduced to a debating society. The awesome power of the CIA and the defense establishment, seem destined to seal the fate of the America I knew as a child and bring us into a new Orwellian world where the citizen exists for the state and where raw power justifies any and every immoral act."

- Jim Garrison, District Attorney, Orleans Parish, LA

Even as America basked in the sunshine of a new-found prosperity in the years following World War II... all was not well in the nation considered to be the leader of the free world. A profound expansion of higher education, driven by the GI Bill... fueled by an unbridled optimism in the decades following the end of the War, was in retrospect, the calm before the storm. There was a growing concern in the mind of then 34th U. S. President, Dwight D Eisenhower... a nagging suspicion was creeping into his consciousness. A suspicion that, given the outcome of WWII, given the growing concern over the USSR and China and the rise of the "Cold War," the "powers that be" in Washington DC were mutating into something beyond the control of traditional political checks and balances.

As the supreme commander of Allied forces in Europe during the war, Eisenhower knew better than most, the ramifications of a changing world. The nation Dwight loved had risen to the challenges of Nazism & Fascism during WWII... had "pulled together" ...militarily in Europe, the South Pacific. On the home front, via the heroic efforts of civilians, as epitomized by "Rosie the Riveter" ...a united America answered the call to defeat the Axis powers.

Even as the Allied forces accepted the surrender of their adversaries on May 7th, 1945, the insidious seed of Nazism & Fascism persisted. Defeated... denounced... dormant... but very much alive. It was as if the fascist seed, trampled under-foot by allied forces, clung to the tread of their military boots marching home... carrying an unexpected and sinister contaminant to American soil.

This contamination first took the form of "Operation Paperclip" which was enacted by Eisenhower's predecessor, 33rd U. S. president, Harry Truman in August of 1945. The Office of Strategic Services (OSS), which later became the CIA, launched Operation Paperclip to recruit Nazi scientists for employment by the United States, thereby denying Nazi technological expertise to the Soviet Union (USSR). Specifically, the OSS was desperate to acquire Nazi rocket scientists and aerospace engineers to monopolize inter-continental weapons delivery and the militarization of space.

The USSR was keenly aware of the strategic ramifications of operation paperclip. The Soviets, via their newly occupied satellite, the German Democratic Republic (East Germany), responded by erecting the "Berlin Wall" in 1961 ...separating Germany's Capitol into East & West Berlin and eliminating access to West Berlin, by land. This was the genesis of the "Cold War" ...a protracted covert campaign of espionage, statesmanship and military brinksmanship, waged between the US and the USSR.

With the Cold War (which lasted overtly until 1991) as a backdrop... the two "superpowers" as they became known, entered into what amounted to a technology war... a race between East & West to achieve technological superiority. In retrospect, the Berlin Airlift, the Korean War, the Cuban missile crisis, mutually assured destruction (MAD), the space race, détente... and finally the demolition of the Berlin Wall *("Mr. Gorbachev, tear down this wall"* – Ronald Reagan, circa 1987) ...all fall into place as pieces of the puzzle that was the "global techno-industrial" clash of superpowers.

The symbolism of the Berlin Wall being the "alpha and omega" of the Cold War is intriguing, given that Germany, now unified and twice rising from the ashes of national defeat and devastation, rose again to become the dominant power of the twenty-first century European Union.

Meanwhile, back on January 17, 1961… a worried President Eisenhower is preparing to leave office by delivering his now famous "Military-Industrial Complex" speech. In this farewell address, Eisenhower predicted and succinctly defined humanity's current socio-political dilemma…

"Until the latest of our world conflicts, the United States had no armaments industry. American makers of plowshares could, with time and as required, make swords as well. But now we can no longer risk emergency improvisation of national defense; we have been compelled to create a permanent armaments industry of vast proportions. Added to this, three and a half million men and women are directly engaged in the defense establishment. We annually spend on military security more than the net income of all United States corporations.

This conjunction of an immense military establishment and a large arms industry is new in the American experience. The total influence… economic, political, even spiritual… is felt in every city, every State house, every office of the Federal government. We recognize the imperative need for this development. Yet we must not fail to comprehend its grave implications. Our toil, resources and livelihood are all involved; so is the very structure of our society.

In the councils of government, we must guard against the acquisition of unwarranted influence, whether sought or unsought, by the military-industrial complex. The potential for the disastrous rise of misplaced power exists and will persist."

- Dwight D Eisenhower, 1961

Prior to the invention and first use of the "Atomic Bomb" in WWII, industries making swords in times of war could make plowshares in times of peace. After WWII, military weaponry became so sophisticated as to require a large complex of industries dedicated solely to its development. Military technologies such as intercontinental missile capability and nuclear weapons gave rise to the modern corporate-controlled State.

The "defense industry," in tandem with an escalating legislative bureaucracy, fed by outrageous sums of money and influence wielded by the fledgling lobbying industry, was the cancerous mutation in

American politics that Ike feared. If left unchecked, Ike implied, the military-industrial complex would become the tyrannical masters of a new world order.

But it was not enough to control governments and economies... these tyrants, via their newly created lackey spook show, the CIA... wanted to control the very minds of their perceived adversaries, as well as... perhaps... the citizenry they were supposed to protect. They not only sought to control outer space, (a nudge from Sputnik 1 in 1957 launched both the space race and the aerospace industry) they planned to control "inner space" as well.

Several secret U.S. government projects grew out of Operation Paperclip. Their purpose was to study mind control, interrogation, behavior modification and related topics. These projects included Project Chatter and Project Bluebird, which was renamed Project Artichoke in 1951. A memorandum from OSS veteran, Richard Helms to CIA director Allen Welsh Dulles indicated Artichoke became Project MK-ULTRA on April 13, 1953.

Project MK-ULTRA was the code name for a covert, illegal CIA human experimentation program, run by the CIA's Office of Scientific Intelligence. MK-ULTRA began in 1953 and continued at least through the late 1960s, and used ordinary citizens, including university students, as its test subjects. Over thirty universities and institutions were involved in this extensive testing and experimentation program, which included covert drug tests on unwitting citizens, Native Americans and foreign nationals. Several of these tests involved the administration of LSD-25 to test subjects in a variety of social situations.

In one such experiment, subjects were given LSD-25 without their knowledge. They were subsequently interrogated under bright lights with doctors in the background taking notes. The subjects were told that their "trips" would be extended indefinitely if they refused to reveal their secrets. People being interrogated in this manner included CIA employees, US military personnel and "agents" suspected of working for the "other side" during the Cold War.

Evidence suggests that a CIA-sponsored MK-ULTRA experiment was conducted at Harvard University from the fall of 1959 through the spring of 1962. Dr Henry Murray, the lead researcher in the Harvard experiment, secured a grant funded by the United States Navy. Murray's Harvard "stress" experiments strongly resembled those run by the OSS, where Murray served during World War II. Twenty two undergraduate students, including Theodore "Unabomber" Kaczynski[18] participated in the Harvard experiments, which were described by some as "disturbing" and "ethically indefensible."

On the West Coast, Oregon author Ken Kesey and singer-songwriter Robert Hunter both volunteered for MK-ULTRA experiments involving LSD-25 and other psychedelic drugs, being carried out through and in association with, Stanford University. Kesey's experiences while under the influence of LSD-25 inspired him to champion the drug outside the confines of the MK-ULTRA experiments, which influenced the early development of the psychedelic counter-culture that was blossoming in San Francisco. Similarly, these experiences were creatively transformative for Hunter:

"Sit back picture yourself swooping up a shell of purple with foam crests of crystal drops soft nigh they fall unto the sea of morning creep-very-softly mist...and then sort of cascade tinkley-bell like (must I take you by the hand, ever so slowly type) and then conglomerate suddenly into a peal of silver vibrant uncomprehendingly, blood singingly, joyously resounding bells... By my faith if this be insanity, then for the love of God permit me to remain insane."

- Robert Hunter

The nefarious initiation by the CIA of the use of such drugs as LSD-25, call into question the very foundation of the psychedelic movement. Indeed, certain conspiracy theories suggest that the sixties counter-revolution was in reality a CIA plot. Regardless, the psychedelic revival did not go as planned by the intelligence community. Although Dr Albert Hoffman's "problem child" ...LSD-25 was clearly the most infamous of substances used by MK-ULTRA, other amazing psychedelics came from odd corners of the natural world...

---

[18] Ted Kaczynski (born May 22, 1942), also known as the "Unabomber," is an American mathematician and serial murderer. He is known for his wide-ranging social critiques, which opposed industrialism and modern technology. Unabomber Manifesto: http://cyber.eserver.org/unabom.txt

"Hofmann created LSD-25 largely out of ergot, a fungus that grows on rye. Mescaline is nothing more than the synthetic essence of peyote cactus. Psilocybin, the drug that Timothy Leary preferred to LSD-25 for his Harvard experiments, was synthesized from exotic Mexican mushrooms that occupy a very special place in CIA history. When the MK-ULTRA team first embarked on its mind-control explorations, the "magic mushroom" was only a rumor or fable to the Western world. On nothing more than the possibility that the legend was based on fact, CIA scientists tracked the mushroom to the most remote parts of Mexico to identify, test and develop its mind-altering properties. The results, like the LSD legacy, were as startling as they were unintended."

"The CIA scientist sent to Mexico in 1953 to investigate such rumors, reported back to headquarters at Langley, VA that he had...

...heard amazing tales about special mushrooms that grew only in the hot and rainy summer months." Such stories had circulated among Europeans in Mexico since Cortez had conquered the country early in the sixteenth century. Spanish friars had reported that the Aztecs used strange mushrooms in their religious ceremonies, which these converters of the heathens described as "demonic holy communions." Aztec priests called the special mushrooms teonanactl, "God's flesh." "But Cortez's plunderers soon lost track of the rite, as did the traders and anthropologists who followed in their wake. Only the legend survived."

- from "Search for the Manchurian Candidate" by John Marks

In 1973 CIA Director Richard Helms ordered all MK-ULTRA files destroyed. Pursuant to this order, most CIA documents regarding the project were destroyed, making a full investigation of MK-ULTRA impossible. Fortunately, a cache of some 20,000 documents survived Helms' purge, as they had been incorrectly stored in a financial record building and were discovered following a "freedom of information act" request in 1977. These documents were fully investigated during Senate Hearings of 1977.

The great irony is that MK-ULTRA and the CIA, in their sinister quest to develop and exploit the ultimate truth serum, (for use against foreign agents, both real and imaginary, as well as paranoia induced domestic threats) were instrumental in "unleashing" these profound substances upon the American public. For these incredibly powerful psychedelics, both synthesized and naturally occurring, to be suddenly made available to the masses, at such a crucial time in American history, seems more than a coincidence.

It has been said that man was invented by water, as a means of transporting itself uphill. Similarly, it is as if these psychedelic substances "had their own agenda" ...for the ways of universe are mysterious indeed. In fact, these psychedelic compounds, as a component (read: intelligence agent) of our mysterious universe, seemed to have found their way, as if "of their own accord," ...to the very people who were ready to receive them. Magic Mushrooms, Peyote and LSD-25 became the Eucharist of the counter-culture that caught fire simultaneously on both the East and West coasts, in the late 1960s.

By their own hands, the tyrant spooks of the military-industrial complex unintentionally ignited a firestorm of psychedelic resistance to their manipulations and control. Blinded by fear, believing their own propaganda, they inadvertently shed light upon their own nefarious activities. The counter-culture of the 1960s, "turned on" by psychedelics, launched the first counterstrike against the Evil Empire. The "Heads" of the counter-culture found strong allies in the civil rights movement and to a great extent spawned the environmental movement.

More significantly, the development of psychedelic culture unique to each coast laid the foundation for the Yankee and Cowboy Psychedelic War that was to be defined by the inner explorations of Leary and company on the East Coast and the antics of Kesey and the Merry Pranksters in the West. Each coast found their unique way in these turbulent times to develop distinct sub-cultures fitting to each coast's character. The Psychedelic counter-culture blossomed, morphed, went underground... but is still with us today. It irreversibly altered our planetary consciousness and started us down the "western road" to enlightenment... in the words of Kesey's Acid Test house band, The Grateful Dead... *"What a long, strange trip it's been."*

It now seems evident that the wide-spread use of psychedelics, such as the technologically manufactured LSD-25 and the naturally occurring Psilocybin mushroom, acted as a "cosmic trigger" for not only the Psychedelic Cowboys and Yankees, but for the world at large. The massive intrusion of psychedelia, in such a pivotal time as the sixties, seems more than a coincidence. In retrospect, it appears to be a catalyst of consciousness... an evolutionary tipping point in human history.

In fact, this author would suggest that the Psychedelic Experience may indeed prove to be an integral *Intelligence Agent* of change, effecting and impacting human consciousness since the dawn of civilization. Within the context of "the truth is far stranger than fiction" …the human/psychoactive substance symbiosis may be even more alien to our normal consciousness than as-yet imagined. As we saw in chapter five, this connection may ultimately lead off-world, in its genesis.

With that said, is the above discourse an avocation of the use of psychoactive substances such as LSD-25?

This author would not dare presume. The life changing, reality altering consequences of consuming so little a volume (only 200 micrograms, in the case of LSD-25) of a substance that is so powerful… so profound… must be the prerogative of the individual. Although various entheogenic substances have been used by humans to explore the psychedelic realm since antiquity, the use of such substances must be carefully considered. Upon this most sensitive topic, this author would defer to Dr Timothy Leary's Two Commandments for the Molecular Age…

1)   *Thou shalt not alter the consciousness of thy fellow man.*

2)   *Thou shalt not prevent thy fellow man from altering his or her own consciousness.*

But should one so choose… Beware!

The ramifications are great… the risks are high… for to do so is to enter Hermann Hesse's Magic Theatre… *for madmen only.* To open the doors of perception in such a manner leads to "Chapel Perilous" …the psychological no-man's land between temporal and meta-consciousness… again, more on this later. As we shall see, the interaction of psychedelic substances with humanity may be a far longer and far stranger trip than is commonly considered.

Given the mythic, religious and historic record, it is evident that psychoactive substances have acted as an evolutionary catalyst for thousands of years… reaching back to humanity's pre-history. Like the nested, intertwining structure of the DNA molecule, the symbiotic intertwining of humanity and psychedelics is clearly evidenced for at least 10,000 years. Psychedelics and humans have been, and are, bound by the same fate.

Coinciding with the rise of psychedelia in the years and decades after WW II, there developed an amazing body of work in the field of Psychology. These works were preceded by the preeminent neurologist, Dr. Sigismund Schlomo Freud... commonly known as Sigmund Freud. Freud is widely credited with being the "founding father" of psychoanalysis. Freud developed therapeutic techniques such as the use of free association, in which patients report their thoughts without reservation and in whichever order they spontaneously occur. From this foundation, archetypical dream-work, a theory of cosmic order and a psychological framework for understanding the human species would emerge.

In our next chapter, we will examine in greater detail, the way seemingly un-related occurrences combined and contributed in a mosaic nexus of meaningful coincidence and how these synchronicities laid the groundwork for the information age to come...

8
SYNCHRONICITY

"Like an island in the sea we appear as distinct individuals, but beneath the surface we are all connected."

- Carl Jung

Another luminary native son of Switzerland (born just 31 years before LSD-25's creator, Dr Albert Hoffman) was the renowned psychiatrist and pioneer psychotherapist: Dr. Carl Gustav Jung. Like Hoffman, Jung's contribution to modern culture continues to exponentially expand in magnitude. His body of work has not only been influential in modern psychiatry, it has had profound influence in the study of religion, philosophy, archeology, anthropology, and literature.

Jung was a close colleague of Dr. Sigmund Freud, who is widely considered to be the founder of psychoanalysis. Jung broke away from the Freudian psychoanalysis school of thought, over the issue of the unconscious mind as a reservoir of repressed sexual trauma which causes all neuroses. Jung believed that the unconscious mind was far more dynamic. Jung founded his own school of analytical psychology or "Jungian Psychology." This discipline examines an individual's psyche, or totality of the mind.

Within Jungian psychology, the psyche manifests as a three-fold interplay, consisting of the Ego, the Individual Unconscious and the Collective Unconscious. Further, Jungian psychology views the integration between an individual's conscious and unconscious mind to be essential to the development of a healthy psyche. In examining and contrasting the conscious and the unconscious mind, it is the unconscious that is considered to be the richer, more active component of mind.

A brief synopsis of the main components of Jungian Psychology, are as follows…

Collective Unconscious

In addition to the individual unconscious, Jungian psychology places great emphasis on the "collective unconscious," or the humanity-wide shared elements of the psyche. Jung coined the term "collective unconscious" to refer to that part of a person's unconscious which is common to all human beings, as opposed to personal unconscious, which is unique to each individual. Jungian psychology contends that the collective unconscious is an integral wellspring of the human psyche. Further, the collective unconscious is inseparable from the individual's psyche.

Jungian Psychology pursues an individual's wholeness through the integration of unconscious forces and motivations underlying human behavior. In order for the individual to achieve wholeness, or to use Jung's phrase… individuation… he/she must incorporate the psyche of the collective… of all humanity. Depth psychology, including archetypal psychology, employs the model of the unconscious mind as the source of healing and development in an individual.

The concept of collective unconscious can be related to the Spiritual (Gnostic) model of living beings consisting of individuated parts of Universal Spirit, encased in physical form. According to Jung, the collective unconscious contains archetypes, which are thought-forms or psychically charged symbols that are manifested by all people in all cultures. The thought-form concept may be somewhat compared with the "Tulpa" …a Tibetan concept of a being or object which is created through sheer spiritual or mental discipline alone. According to the 20th century Belgian-French explorer & spiritualist, Alexandra David-Néel… Tulpas are "magical formations, generated by a powerful concentration of thought."

Archetypes

Within Jung's interpretation, archetypes (thought-forms) are inherent prototypes for ideas, which may subsequently become relevant or conceptually involved in the interpretation of observed phenomena. A group of memories and interpretations closely associated with an archetype is called a complex, and may be named for its central archetype (e.g. Freud's "oedipus complex"). Jung often seemed to view the archetypes as psychological organs, directly analogous to our physical, bodily organs... both being morphological givens for the species; both arising (at least partially) through evolutionary processes. There are four famous forms of archetypes identified by Jung:

The Self ...the unification of consciousness and unconsciousness in a person, and representing the psyche as a whole.

The Shadow ...every manifest part of ourselves has a repressed and opposite counterpart, represented by the shadow.

The Anima ...feminine principal, a young lady, representing intuitive wisdom.

The Animus ...masculine principal, a handsome young man, representing active, assertive energy.

Archetypical symbols of the unconscious mind abound in Jungian psychology. For example: The Syzygy (Divine Couple), The Child, The Superman, The Hero, The Great Mother (manifested either as the Good Mother or the Terrible Mother), The Wise Old Man, The Trickster or Ape.

Similar to Tulpas, the visualization or verbalization of Jung's archetypes may be associated with the concept of "sigils" or occult symbols... ie: ideas and images that have become charged with significance through eons of reflection and veneration, now standing ready to release their collective potential, upon invocation. In Jungian terms, this invocation becomes the conscious pursuit of individuation.

For example, Jung interpreted the "Ouroboros" or the image of a snake biting its own tail, as having an archetypical significance to the human psyche. It represents the integration and assimilation of the opposite, i.e. of the shadow. The Jungian psychologist Erich Neumann further defined the ouroboros as a representation of the pre-ego "dawn state", depicting the (as yet) undifferentiated infancy experience of both mankind and the individual child.

Historically, the ouroboros is a key symbol associated with the ancient, heretical and mystical pre-Christian sects, whose philosophy has since been collectively referred to as "Gnosticism." The following is from an Apocryphal, or non-canonical esoteric text...

"I am eternal change. As I devour my tail I am the eternal in constant becoming. Study my coiling and by the torturous path you will return to the I in One."

- The Book of Adamas

Jung's premise of archetypes, as they pertain to the individuation or wholeness of consciousness of the self, pointed to a deeper level of universal consciousness. Humanity's use of language was an artifact, a contrivance, sigil or tool that assisted humanity in the realization of that shared consciousness. Per Jung:

"Language is originally and essentially nothing but a system of signs or symbols, which denote real occurrences, or their echo in the human soul."

Synchronicity

Jung coined the term synchronicity to describe the alignment of "universal forces" with the life experiences of an individual. Jung believed that many experiences perceived as coincidences were not merely due to chance, but instead reflected the creation of an event or circumstance by the "coinciding" or alignment of such forces. Again, the process of becoming intuitively aware and acting in harmony with these forces is what Jung labeled "individuation". Jung maintained that an individuated person would actually shape events around them through the communication of their consciousness with the collective unconscious. In other words: an interface between the individual and universe.

This concept mirrors the ancient Asian conception of universal force, referred to as the "Tao" ...an ancient Chinese concept signifying the 'way', 'path' or 'route.' The name Tao is used to describe the primordial essence or fundamental nature of the universe. From the classic Tao te Ching:

"The Tao is described as the Mysterious Mother:
Empty yet inexhaustible, it gives birth to infinite worlds.
It is always present within & without you.
It is the root of Heaven and Earth."

Like the Tao within Taoist thought and the Holy Ghost, in Gnostic understanding, synchronicity is an expression of the sublime, ineffable fabric that connects humanity. It is a manifestation of a vast network of universal communication (referred to within Tek-Gnostics mythology as: The Matrix). Beyond psychically linking humanity to one another, synchronicity is an expression of humanity's intimate connectedness to universe.

Although Jung identified the psyche as mind, he also recognized the mystery of soul. Jung considered the world of dream, myth, and folklore to be a promising and necessary road to deeper understanding and meaning. He considered the practice of exploring the accumulative phenomenology that included the significance of dreams, archetypes and mythology, to be valid additions to the body of empirical evidence within the study of psychology.

The accomplished mythologist, Joseph Campbell built upon the work of Jung to illustrate the archetypical underpinnings of ancient stories and myths. Campbell's understanding of myth aligns with the Jungian method of dream interpretation, which is heavily dependent upon symbolic interpretation. In turn, Jung's insights into archetypes were heavily influenced by the ancient *Tibetan Book of the Dead* (Bardo Thodol).[19] In Campbell's book: *The Mythic Image* (1974), he quotes Jung, that the Bardo Thodol ...

"Belongs to that class of writings which not only are of interest to specialists in Mahayana Buddhism, but also, because of their deep humanity and still deeper insight into the secrets of the human psyche, make an especial appeal to the layman seeking to broaden his knowledge of life... For years, ever since it was first published, the Bardo Thodol has been my constant companion, and to it I owe not only many stimulating ideas and discoveries, but also many fundamental

---

[19] See: https://en.wikipedia.org/wiki/Bardo_Thodol

insights."

Campbell's conception of a global "Monomyth" …that all mythic narratives are variations of a single great story, informed his life-long study of world mythologies. Campbell's theory is based upon the observation that commonalities exist beneath the narrative elements of most great myths, regardless of their origin.

Interestingly, Campbell's first major published work was: *A Skeleton Key to Finnegans Wake* (1944). Co-written with Henry Morton Robinson, this work is a critical analysis of the great Irish author, James Joyce's epic: *Finnegans Wake* (1939). It is intriguing that Campbell credits Joyce's Wake… which is arguably the greatest work of modern English literature, as a profound inspiration. In fact, Campbell's conception of the monomyth… or the cycle of the journey of the hero… is a term that he lifted directly from Joyce's Wake. The synchronicities deepen for the purposes of this work, as the work of Marshall McLuhan, outlined in chapter three, was also greatly inspired by James Joyce. McLuhan especially referenced Finnegans Wake throughout his collage book: *War and Peace in the Global Village* (1968).

Informed by Jung, Campbell's work on mythology continues to influence contemporary storytellers. In an article entitled: *A Practical Guide to Joseph Cambell's The Hero with a Thousand Faces* …Hollywood consultant Christopher Vogler suggested the connection between archetype and myth extends to modern story telling through film…

"…Campbell's thinking runs parallel to that of Swiss psychologist Carl Jung, who wrote of the archetypes as constantly repeating characters, who occur in the dreams of all people and in the myths of all cultures. Jung suggested that these archetypes are reflection of aspects of the human mind… that our personalities divide themselves into these characters to play out the drama of our lives. He noticed a strong correspondence between his patients' dream or fantasy figures and the common archetypes of mythology, and he suggested that both were coming from a deeper source, in the "collective unconscious" of the human race.

The repeating characters of the hero myth such as the young hero, the wise old man or woman, the shape-shifting woman or man, and the shadowy antagonist are identical with the archetypes of the human mind, as revealed in dreams. That's why myths, and stories constructed on the mythological model, strike us as psychologically true. Such stories are true models of the workings of the human mind, true maps of the psyche. They are psychologically valid and realistic even when they portray fantastic, impossible, unreal events. The myth is easily translated to contemporary dramas, comedies, romances, or action-adventures by substituting modern equivalents for the symbolic figures and props of the hero story."

- Christopher Vogler

Vogler's insight is clearly evidenced in many popular (and commercially successful) motion pictures, such as the archetypically rich *Star Wars* (original trilogy) films. Luke Skywalker as the young hero, Obi-Wan Kenobi as the wise old man, even Han Solo's sidekick, Chewbacca can be compared to the wildman, or ape archetype. The continued success of this franchise, which has infatuated our pop-culture since 1977, draws attention to the deep resonance that this modernized mythology has had on our contemporary collective unconscious.

Jung's approach has not only been influential in the field of psychology, it has proved to play a prominent and formative role in countercultural movements across the globe. Jung is considered as the first modern psychologist to state that the human psyche is "by nature, religious" and to explore this concept in depth. He emphasized understanding the psyche through exploring the worlds of dreams, art, mythology, religion and philosophy.

Although he was a theoretical psychologist and practicing clinician, much of his life's work was spent exploring other areas, including Eastern and Western philosophy, alchemy, astrology, sociology, as well as literature and the arts. Little wonder his most notable ideas included the concept of psychological archetypes, synchronicity and the collective unconscious. In Jung's words…

"There are no longer any gods whom we can invoke to help us. The great religions of the world suffer from increasing anaemia because the helpful numina have fled from the woods, rivers, mountains, and animals, and the God-men have disappeared underground into the unconscious. There we suppose they lead an ignominious existence among the relics of the past, while we remain dominated by the great 'Déesse Raison' …who is our overwhelming illusion. We are so captivated by and entangled in our subjective consciousness that we have simply forgotten the age-old fact that God speaks chiefly through dreams and visions. Whatever else the unconscious may be, it is a natural phenomenon that produces

symbols, and these symbols prove to be meaningful.

At a time when all available energy is spent in the investigation of nature, very little attention is paid to the essence of human-kind, which is psyche, although many researches are made into its conscious functions. But the really unknown part, which produces symbols, is still virtually unexplored. We receive signals from it every night (Dreaming) yet deciphering these communications seems to be such an odious task that very few people in the whole civilized world can be bothered with it. Humankind's greatest instrument, psyche, is little thought of, if not actually mistrusted and despised.

This modern standpoint is surely one-sided and unjust. It does not even accord with the known facts. Our actual knowledge of the unconscious shows it to be a natural phenomenon, and that, like nature herself, it is at least neutral. It contains all aspects of human nature... light and dark, beautiful and ugly, good and evil, profound and silly. The study of individual as well as collective symbolism is an enormous task, and one that has not yet been mastered. But at last a beginning has been made. The results so far gained are encouraging, and they seem to indicate an answer to many of the questions perplexing present-day humankind."

One of Jung's final essays was titled: *Flying Saucers: A Modern Myth of Things Seen in the Skies* (with RCF Hull, 1979). In keeping with the synchronous nature of this narrative, it is no surprise that Jung would find interest in the emerging UFO phenomena:

"Rather than assuming that the modern prevalence of UFO sightings are due to extraterrestrial craft, Jung reserves judgment on their origin & connects UFOs with archetypal imagery, concluding that they have become a "living myth." This essay is intriguing in its methodology & implications as to the nature of UFOs & their relation to the human psyche."

Within Tek-Gnostics cosmology, Jung's Synchronicity is not merely a term used to describe meaningful coincidence; it is also a communicative mode... a conduit... a medium whereby the interconnectedness of all things, separated as they are by time and space... occur. If modern understandings of time and space are to be perceived as outer-dimensional constants, so too must Jung's understanding of "meaning" be perceived as an inner-dimensional constant... operating outside the confines of space/time.

Simply stated, Synchronicity is a universal mechanism of meaning.

Synchronicity is a "cosmic trigger" that is evidenced by those who recognize it for what it is... the "perceived" manifestation of communion between self and universe. It is the observable demonstration of "non-local" interaction between seemingly separate entities... again, independent of, or not affected by, time and space.

Synchronicity is a physical expression of the interconnectedness of universe, on the pure consciousness level of reality. It is the "medium of magic" wherein events that were historically considered miraculous, are facilitated. It is the mechanism through which paranormal ability and "psi" phenomena exist and operate. It is the active instrument through which creativity is sparked. It is also the medium, the filament through which creativity flows.

In this regard, synchronicity behaves as a creative field of energy... permeating universe... that can be tapped into by receptive beings. Similar in concept to Rupert Sheldrake's[20] "Morphic Resonance" theory, synchronicity is the networked "universal force" that Jung consistently referred to. It is popularly exemplified in "the force" within the above mentioned Star Wars mythology. An illustration of this principle, in the creative sense, is the apparent "coincidence" of two individuals coming up with the same idea, at the same moment.

In archetypical fashion, the ancient Greeks deified and named this creative principle "The Muses." Within Greek mythology, the Muses were traditionally depicted as the nine daughters of Zeus and Mnemosyne (who was memory personified). Archetypically, the Muses were the personification of knowledge and the arts, especially literature, dance and music.

Finally, synchronicity can be considered a "mythic metric" or unit of measurement. In this case, it measures the frequency of instances of meaningful coincidence. It is the repeated experience of "Déjà vu." It is the flash of 11:11[21] on your electronic devices. It is a common occurrence for those who study synchronicity to experience an increase in frequency of these synchronistic events. It can be argued that, like conspiracy theory, once an individual begins to look for coincidence, they see it everywhere... just as when one purchases a VW beetle, they begin to see "slug bugs" everywhere on the road.

This "self-fulfilling prophecy" criticism is likely true, but it

---

[20] See: https://en.wikipedia.org/wiki/Rupert_Sheldrake
[21] See for instance: https://en.wikipedia.org/wiki/11:11_(numerology)

doesn't diminish the "meaning" of meaningful coincidence, for those who experience synchronicity… for it is in the perceived meaning, within the individual's consciousness, that synchronicity's value resides. As a metric of meaningful coincidence, synchronicity can be perceived as an indicator of humanities' cumulative paranormal development… a threshold or "hundredth monkey"[22] indicator.

Jung developed the theories of psychological archetypes, synchronicity and the collective unconscious as a framework or model of the continuity, the eternal unfolding, of universe. He had experienced the interconnectedness of all that is, and began to formulate… to codify… to map, if you will… this vast, limitless territory. He knew from his experience that the inner world of human consciousness was inseparable from the outer, material world.

He perceived that separation in space and time did not appear to be an inhibiting factor in the workings of synchronicity. These connections occur, no matter the distance. Within the associative concept of synchronicity and time, the emphasis is on "timing" …or the art of regulating actions in order to achieve the best result …not simply the passage of time. This distinction is what puts the "meaning" in meaningful coincidence.

Jung's understandings align nearly perfectly with the pop-psychedelic consciousness that reemerged in the Western World in the sixties. In synchronistic terms, it was no coincidence that the psychological framework of Jung found popularity in the West, essentially at the same time as Hoffman's problem child …LSD-25. The two artifacts combine… intertwine… to form a complete contemporary psychedelic cosmology.

Hoffman's creation was the physical catalyst, while Jung's, creation was the symbolic framework. Hoffman synthesized a chemical that profoundly acted upon the mind, while Jung developed a conceptual structure that profoundly influenced psychological thinking. Hoffman provided the "How" …and Jung provided the "Why."

---

[22] See: https://en.wikipedia.org/wiki/Hundredth_monkey_effect

9
INTELLIGENCE ENGINEERING

"In the province of the mind, what one believes to be true either is true or becomes true."

- John C Lilly

Returning to that pivotal and synchronistic "Summer of Love" year... in his pioneering 1967 dissertation: *Programming and Metaprogramming in the Human Biocomputer: Theory and Experiments* ...Dr. John C Lilly postulated that humans are essentially a "biological computer," born with specific bio-firmware programming such as eating, sleeping, and feeling pain... embedded in their DNA's genetic code. Our ability to take in new information and to develop ideas beyond these innate programs depends upon our capacity for "meta-programming," or learning to learn.

Building upon the contemporary psychological and psychedelic cosmology of Dr Carl G Jung... as chemically exemplified by Dr Albert Hoffman's "problem child," Dr Lilly set about creating a non-chemical alternative... a "how to" protocol for the emerging psychedelic consciousness paradigm. If LSD-25 knocked down the "Doors of Perception," Lilly's work sought a "skeleton key" to unlock the psychedelic experience. Along with many others, Lilly began to develop a system of consciousness expansion that did not rely upon the (often traumatic) ingestion of a chemical compound.

Lilly's deep interest in the workings of consciousness led to his research in sensory deprivation via his development of the isolation tank. While employed by the National Institute of Mental Health, Lilly designed this technology to isolate the human brain from all other external stimuli. Through sensory deprivation, Lilly sought to access the psychedelic experience by minimizing stimulus to the five senses, thereby unleashing the "sixth sense.".

Lilly's research soon began to integrate and incorporate Eastern as well as Western consciousness technologies. Lilly studied Patanjali's[23] system of yoga. He also explored Self-enquiry meditation, as advocated by Ramana Maharshi.[24] After extensive investigations, Lilly came to the conclusion that I. K. Taimni's[25] Science of Yoga, a modernized interpretation of the Sanskrit text, most closely aligned with his understandings.

Additionally, Lilly pioneered interspecies communication with his life-long passion for higher marine mammals, specifically his work with dolphins. His scientific understanding was that, aside from the human brain, the dolphin's brain is the most powerful and complex brain of all mammals. Consequently, Lilly's approach to intelligence research transcended humanity to encompass multiple earthling species.

Add to these divergent disciplines, Lilly's contributions to computer science and his founding role in SETI[26] (search for extra-terrestrial intelligence), and a truly universal understanding of... not merely intelligence, but consciousness... begins to emerge. With the founding of SETI, the modern scientific search for off-world consciousness and extra-terrestrial intelligences began.

Lilly's work coincided with the emergence of the "Human Potential Movement," itself an outgrowth of the socio-cultural environment that was incubating in the sixties. The human potential movement has been associated with humanistic psychology, as initially popularized by the work of Abraham Maslow[27] (Although Maslow advocated a "strength based" approach to psychological development, his work has more recently been criticized for cultural bias). Lilly sought a more integrative, physiological, psychological,

---

[23] See: https://en.wikipedia.org/wiki/Yoga_Sutras_of_Patanjali
[24] See: https://en.wikipedia.org/wiki/Ramana_Maharshi
[25] See: https://en.wikipedia.org/wiki/I._K._Taimni
[26] See: https://en.wikipedia.org/wiki/Search_for_extraterrestrial_intelligence
[27] See: https://en.wikipedia.org/wiki/Abraham_Maslow

even spiritual approach to human potential.

Lilly's multi-faceted work in consciousness exploration served to provide the finishing touch that transformed the psychedelic revolution into a spiritual and intellectual basis for a psychedelic cultural cosmology. Like a cosmic recipe, his vision brought together the essential ingredients... a pinch of computer science, a dash of psychology, a teaspoon of psychedelics, eastern teachings, environmentalism, even a touch of the logical consideration of extraterrestrial intelligence... all combined in just the right proportions.

Psychedelic Engineers

So it was from this psychedelic cosmology, as informed by the psychological work of Jung and the psychedelic work of Hoffman... that a unique faction of consciousness explorers or what we refer to as: "Psychedelic Engineers" emerged from the rapidly expanding human potential movement. Unlike the main body of the human potential movement, which quickly de-generated into a mish-mash of pop psychology, self-help, abundance attraction and life coaching (not that there's anything wrong with that!), the Psychedelic Engineering faction sought a cutting-edge blend of science and spiritualism.

At the time, this faction... in addition to Lilly... included in part, such disparate characters as psychologist Timothy Leary, et al (East Coast Cabal) novelist Ken Kesey and the Pranksters (West Coast Cabal) William S Burroughs, Hunter S Thompson and Alan Watts, etc. These counter-cultural icons, along with (then) relative newcomers, such as Robert Anton Wilson, Philip K Dick and Terence McKenna, seemed about as "fringy" as it gets. But there was a method to their madness.

Leary went on to popularize (and "Westernize") an obscure tantric manuscript that blended eastern teachings of the human "chakra" system, with western psychological equivalents. This model of consciousness originally known as "Neurologic" soon became popularly known as the *Eight Brain Model of Consciousness* which was instrumental in defining the philosophic foundation of the ensuing "cyberpunk" culture. Leary's brilliance was in the integration of the Eastern Hindu and Tantric teachings with Western Psychology and Psychedelic inner exploration. Leary's Eight Brain Model continues to attract a cult-like following, to this day.

Having been "experienced" via the MK-Ultra trials at Stanford… Kesey, along with the pranksters, developed a psychedelic freak-out, love-in, mind-theatre of "Higher" education and assessment, known as the Acid Tests. Kesey would provide physical transport via his now-famous school bus. Beyond the realm of the material, Kesey would provide inner, psychedelic transport via LSD-25. Just like the name Kesey gave to his day-glow festooned school bus, he sought to take the emerging psychedelic culture… Further.

Kesey facilitated and presided over the Acid Tests during the autumn of 1965 and throughout 1966. Interestingly, he ended the two-year Acid-test curriculum on October 31st, on the day of the ancient pagan harvest festival, Samhain, or All Hallow's Eve, now known as "Halloween" …with an Acid Test Graduation, performed at San Francisco's infamous rock concert venue, the Winterland Ballroom. This graduation foreshadowed the "Death of the Hippie" dirge, led by the improvisational collective, *the Diggers,* in the fall of 1967.

Co-conspirators: Burroughs, Thompson and Watts all contributed in their unique fashion to the rapidly expanding psychedelic culture. Burroughs' *Naked Lunch* (1959) and Thompson's *Fear & Loathing* (1972) series, examined such topics as contemporary politics, consensual reality, gender and the nature of madness, within the psychedelic perspective. Watts took the more disciplined path of Zen, a school of Mahayana Buddhism. His book: *The Way of Zen* (1957) introduced the sixties youth culture to Zen's snarky, no-nonsense approach to philosophy.

The prolific science fiction writer, Philip K Dick examined multiple, often colliding realities. Dick's neo-Gnostic, sci-fi writings were heavily influenced by the contemporary psychedelic scene, as well as the writings of Carl Jung. The Jungian constructs and models that intrigued Dick were the archetypes of the collective unconscious, group projection and/or hallucination and synchronicity.

Like Dick, newcomer Terence McKenna was influenced by Carl Jung at an early age. It is reported that McKenna read Jung's book: *Psychology and Alchemy* (1968) at the age of 10. McKenna's *True Hallucinations: Being an Account of the Author's Extraordinary Adventures in the Devil's Paradise* (1993) is an autobiographical recounting of Terence McKenna's psychedelic communion with psilocybin mushrooms in the Amazon Basin.

This brings us to the final Psychedelic Engineer within our cabal of consciousness... Robert Anton Wilson. Although Wilson may not be as renowned or notorious (depending upon one's perspective), as the others on our list, his body of work most closely captured the irreverent, entertaining, yet well considered spirit of the era. Wilson's works, as epitomized by: *Cosmic Trigger: The Final Secret of the Illuminati* (1977) bridged a generational gap to the next evolutionary step in consciousness exploration.

Wilson's writings were steeped in the psychedelic sensibilities of the sixties, yet they pioneered a genre of literary style that resonated with the next generation of psychedelic culture. The biological offspring of the first psychedelic generation (the flower children or hippies) demonstrated a "swing of the pendulum" in cultural responsiveness. This next gen. included a no-nonsense, Avant Garde, tech-savvy faction of intellectual rebellion, known as "Cyberpunk."

Cyberpunk is most commonly considered a subgenre of science fiction, usually set in a dystopian near-future, characterized by extensive human interaction with supercomputers and infused with punk ambiance. As we have since seen, life imitates art. With the rise of the Anonymous[28] phenomena in the first decade of the 21st Century, yesterday's science fiction becomes today's reality.

Wilson commentated and expanded upon the work of Leary (who also embraced the cyberpunk ethic) in such a way as to be palatable to the cynical sensibilities of the world's first computer-literate generation. Specifically, he expanded upon Leary's Eight Brain model, now reworked and repackaged as the *Eight Circuit Model of Consciousness,* using computer science analogies that resonated with the cyberpunks.

As a result, the meditative, heavy-water lightshow, Hari Krishna consciousness of the sixties, transformed into the fractally expanding, "consciousness hacking," virtual reality of the 90's. This cyberpunk ethos is still with us today, not merely with the Anonymous collective, but with the erosion of western culture, as prophesized in the classic cyberpunk novels of the 80's, such as Dick's *Radio Free Albermuth* (published posthumously in 1985). We currently appear to live in the very dystopian world envisioned all those decades ago.

---

[28] Anonymous (used as a mass noun) is a loosely associated international network of activist and hacktivist entities.

The psychedelic engineers, as dissimilar as they appear... all were seeking technologies, both material and conceptual, that would facilitate a broader understanding and distribution of the psychedelic revolution. They sought mechanisms of conveyance, systems of teaching... they sought individually or in concert, to create a how-to manual of psychedelic enlightenment. Their intent was to make the profound realizations of the emerging psychedelic culture available to all.

Consciousness Hacking

Fast Forward. The world in which we live today is amazing, indeed... filled with technological marvel. Few, back in the sixties, predicted the rise of the personal computer and how thoroughly it would change our world. In fact, our modern technologies are so advanced from those used by NASA in our 1969 manned moon landing, that they nearly fulfill Arthur C Clark's famous third law. Strangely, amidst this age of miracle and wonder, a tech-driven eschatological angst creeps into our collective consciousness...

As introduced in chapter one, it has been argued by scientists, futurists and those who consider such things, that within thirty years we will have the technological means to create superhuman artificial intelligence. The concept has been given the popular title... *Technological Singularity*, or simply... Singularity.

The analogy to the black hole phenomena references the fact that prognosticating what the future might look like after AI/human parity is essentially unpredictable. No light of recognition escapes from this technological singularity threshold. The concern that has been raised by contemporary tech gurus is essentially that, at the moment when our computing technology (AI) surpasses our own intelligence capacity... at the moment of singularity... the human era will come to a close.

The fear-based technological eschatology inferred in the above is but the latest manifestation of a deep, dark and recurring collective phobia. Within Christian eschatology, this phenomenon is known as "end-times prophesy." The Twentieth Century's scientific version of the "end of the world as we know it" was known as the Y2K bug. As the millennium approached, a calendar date programming glitch in computing systems, both personal and mainframe, threatened to cause digital devastation across the globe.

The "new-age" version of this was, of course, the 2012 Mayan Calendar prophecy, as popularized by José Argüelles and among others, the afore-mentioned Terence McKenna, in his novelty theory and subsequent "Timewave Zero"[29] software. Like so many other prophecies of doom, the havoc that was predicted did not come to pass (as of yet). The latest and greatest version of scientific end-times eschatology, the twenty-first century version, is none other than... *technological singularity.* Although singularity has been framed in scientific verbiage, it is reasonable to view these fears as eschatological, or religious, in nature. This is in keeping with the understanding that from the tekgnostic perspective, science can be considered humanity's most recent religion.

As indicated in chapter one, there are a variety of scenarios whereby the moment of singularity comes about. Computer networks and human-computer interfaces, one of humanity's more recent and spectacular artifacts, may be instrumental in what has been titled *Intelligence Amplification* (IA). Also referred to as "cognitive augmentation," IA refers to the effective use of information technology in augmenting human intelligence. Consciously disallowing fear and proceeding from a "cup half full" perspective, this book proposes that we collectively choose to synergistically participate in the singularity mythology, in a way that is beneficial for humanity and Gaia[30] our home world.

Emergent developments in artificial intelligence will no-doubt impact Intelligence Amplification, and vice versa. With that said, humanity needs to recognize that in "Deep Learning" or artificial neural network and interface research, there is the immanent possibility of a thing as profound and potentially sentient as a human intelligence amplified Artificial Intelligence partnership. With that insight, we may see the internet, a mundane interface and networking tool, serve to advance us toward the singularity along the networked, IA path... thereby creating a human/technological planetary grid... a true, technologically assisted global sentience.

---

[29] See for instance...
https://en.wikipedia.org/wiki/Timewave_zero#Novelty_theory_and_Timewave_Zero
[30] The personification of Earth in ancient Greek mythology. Also, see:
ttps://en.wikipedia.org/wiki/Gaia_hypothesis

We therefore consciously choose to participate in a singularity process, a "consciousness hacking" process, if you will... that facilitates Intelligence Amplification as opposed to a strict Artificial Intelligence option. Computer networks and human-computer interfaces are more accessible than AI and as an infrastructure, are already in place. As Vernor Vinge indicated, every time our ability to access information and to communicate it to other humans is improved, we have achieved a technologically assisted augment over natural intelligence.

It is fitting that we use the technological analogy of "hacking" consciousness to examine the concept of Intelligence Amplification. IA intimately includes the active human participant or hacker, in the AI equation. In the ambition of successfully partnering with AI, let us turn our attention to those intrepid individuals who would hack our emerging technologically assisted global sentience...

The Intelligence Engineers

The marvelous opportunity presented by the world-wide-web is that it is remotely participatory. As the cost comes down and access by a greater portion of humanity increases, the web also becomes more proletariat. As connectivity, bandwidth, archive size and computer speed all increase, we are experiencing the transformation of our very biosphere into a vast data processor, with a million times greater speed and with millions of human intelligent agents in direct participation. It is the individual intelligent agent, working consciously within the global nerve-net, that is, by this book's definition: the *Intelligence Engineer.*

We define the processes whereby an individual, having a working knowledge of and possessing the capability to modify, augment and increase his or her own intelligence and consciousness, as: *Intelligence Engineering* (iE). By altering the brain's normal operations via the application of various Intelligence Engineering techniques, the range of human thought, the power and ability of the human mind can be increased beyond any previous expectation.

Again, humans-as-tool-builders create artifacts, both physical and conceptual. These artifacts, within the context of intelligence engineering, take the form of language, epic tale, the written word, books, libraries, computer databanks, the internet, etc. They also take the form of ancient yogas, Sūtras, mantra and tantra, ritual, spiritual exercise, logic, intuition, etc. These are all part of the human interface with Gaia... global and universal sentience.

These artifacts, physical and conceptual, represent the tools or technologies available to us, as intelligence engineers. We utilize these various tools to explore the limits of... and to augment... our consciousness. Taken together in the pursuit of inner exploration and intelligence amplification, this "toolbox" of consciousness enhancement... is our TEK.

We pursue consciousness exploration, like those before us, out of a sense of curiosity and awe, as to the wondrous workings of universe. We yearn to increase our knowledge of universe and our place within it. Often, in the pursuit of such knowledge, culminating circumstances produce, transmit or project incredible moments of revelation or insight upon our consciousness. The sudden flash of insight, resulting from our inquiry, often by means of our TEK... the resulting "ah-ha!" moment or epiphany... is our GNOSIS.

Hence, we define Tek-Gnostics as: *The balanced application of artifact and epiphany...*

Returning to consciousness hacking... it can be defined as an enthusiastic and skillful meta-programming of the human bio-firmware. This inner programming is enhanced by the Intelligence Engineer, or meta-programmer... one who studies the art of learning. The consciousness hacking ethos is infused with a passionate curiosity the French have so eloquently called: "amateurism." The word amateur is literally translated as "lover of" which, rather than indicating a lack of expertise, instills a crucial, creative sense of passion in the process.

Again, as we have seen, modern hacking has taken on a socially conscious, politically savvy quality. Archetypically, the hacker takes on aspects of Jung's Hero... the intrepid individual, ragging against the machine... having at their disposal wondrous trinkets and amulets that allow access to a magical realm. This modern mythology is conducive to the western world's (capitalist) ideal of rugged individualism.

Rugged individualism is all good and well, as far as it goes. However, the western concept of individualism reflects an overtly limited and intellectually shallow understanding of Jung's "individuation" process. Western culture has glorified the individual, which works well for capitalist overlords, hawking pharmaceuticals and beauty products. Within the discipline of Tek-Gnostics... we seek the deeper, intuitive understandings of the workings of universe and the human interface, thereof.

Tek-Gnostics' operational system of Intelligence Engineering, takes as its philosophic framework the new (and improved!) Eight-Fold Path of enlightenment. This conceptual skeletal structure incorporates simultaneously the new-earth technological artifact of the Eight-Circuit Model, as espoused by Leary, Wilson, et al... and the ancient Noble Eight-Fold Path of old-earth... best typified and eloquently illustrated by none other than one of earth's original Intelligence Engineers, the enlightened one, Siddhārtha Gautama... aka: the Buddha.

In difference to certain esoteric schools of the orient, we incorporate an ancient oracular artifact, the *I-Ching*. Also known as the *Book of Changes*, the *I-Ching* is itself an eight-fold apparatus or mechanism, issuing from the original Eight Bagua[31] (eight symbols) that illuminates synchronicity. The philosophic glue that holds our aggregated framework together is a remarkable little text, of ancient origin, attributed to one (mythological?) "Lao Tzu" ...known as the *Tao Te Ching*. This book is arguably the foundation of the quintessential Eastern school of thought known as: "Taoism."

Along with the occidental Gnostic sensibility that illustrates the insanity of any religious structure that allows for massive death and destruction in its name, we choose the above teachings, both ancient and modern, for their compassion, logic and humble self-awareness. Aggregating these sources, philosophic traditions of the past combine to provide a modern global perspective. In keeping with networking technologies utilized by popular on-line aggregated RSS[32] feeds, the Intelligence Engineer "surfs" massive data streams.

So it is that the Intelligence Engineer interacts with his/her world in a deliberate and conscious manner. He or she works in cohort, with her or his peers, as exemplified in modern social media and peer-to-peer file sharing protocols. This individualized, yet group driven system furthers the tekgnostic knowledge base, while taking

---

[31] See: https://en.wikipedia.org/wiki/Bagua
[32] See: https://en.wikipedia.org/wiki/RSS

advantage of economy of scale. This symmetry demonstrates that the experience of the whole is greater than the sum-total of its parts.

In an increasingly networked world, this aggregated approach becomes the de facto communicative modality of the "Century of Singularity." As this emerging communicative modality attracts ever-increasing numbers, our intrepid Intelligence Engineers become the vanguard of an approaching global consciousness. In the next chapter, we will focus in greater detail upon the workings of the noble eight-fold path...

10
THE EIGHT-FOLD PATH

One of his students asked the Buddha... Are you the messiah?
"No," ...answered Buddha. Then are you a healer?
"No," ...Buddha replied.
Then are you a teacher? ...the student persisted.
"No, I am not a teacher."
Then what are you? ...asked the exasperated student.
"I am awake" ...Buddha replied.

- Circa 500 BCE

The Noble Eight-Fold Path is one of the (four) principal teachings of the Buddha, who described it as the way leading to the cessation of suffering and the achievement of self-awakening. It is used to develop insight into the true nature of existence and to eradicate greed, hatred, and delusion. The *Nagara Sutta* is an ancient Buddhist text (sutra), describing, through narrative and parable, the nature of Buddha...

"In the same way I saw an ancient path, an ancient road, traveled by the Rightly Self-awakened Ones of former times. And what is that ancient path, that ancient road, traveled by the Rightly Self-awakened Ones of former times? Just this noble eightfold path: right view, right aspiration, right speech, right action, right livelihood, right effort, right mindfulness, right concentration... I followed that

path. Following it, I came to direct knowledge of the origination of aging & death, direct knowledge of the cessation of aging & death and direct knowledge of the path leading to the cessation of aging & death... Knowing that directly, I have revealed it to monks, nuns, male lay followers & female lay followers..."

- Nagara Sutta

So does the above passage from an ancient Buddhist Sutra attribute (the most recent) Buddha's description of the Noble Eight-fold path. Although referred to as steps along a path, it is not meant as a sequential learning process, but as eight facets of existence, each to be integrated in everyday life. Thus the eight facets of seeking enlightenment are comprised of:

1) Right understanding,
2) Right motives,
3) Right speech,
4) Right action,
5) Right means of livelihood,
6) Right effort,
7) Right intellectual activity, and
8) Right contemplation.

Taken together, these eight facets act as an essential field guide to mindful living.

It is with the highest and most profound regard, that we typify Buddha as one of Earth's greatest Intelligence Engineers. He dedicated his life to the pursuit and development of a modality to assist others in fully activating their perceptive faculties or in his words... in "waking up." Even as we attribute the noble eight-fold path (N8P) to Buddha, remember that Buddha himself attributes his re-discovery of the N8P to earlier Buddhas, who themselves re-discovered it, ad infinitum. Thus we carry forward the N8P, adding to its foundation: the Eight Circuit Model of Consciousness.

The Eight Circuits

I first came across the eight circuit or "8 brain model" while reading Robert Anton Wilson's: *The Illuminati Papers* (1980). Wilson had in turn credited Timothy Leary, Ph.D. for creating this mode/tool for understanding the human nervous system. There is evidence that suggests Leary received this information in the form of an obscure manuscript, penned by a Tantric Yoga Master in India, from a mysterious intermediary: "Professor Adams." Regardless of origination, Leary integrated the Eastern Hindu and Tantric teachings with Western Psychology and Psychedelic inner exploration, writing several books on the subject, such as *Exo-Psychology* (1977).

The eight-circuit model of consciousness is not only a system used for understanding the human nervous system, it is a tool used to accelerate human consciousness. It aligns or overlays, as metaphor, with the ancient Hindu chakra grid/system of the human body. Understanding and use of this model assumes that the mind/brain consists of the entire nervous, lymph and circulatory system within the earthling body. Physical, physiological as well as emotional attributes are contained within this system.

Imagine eight subtle spiraling wheels of energy, one above the other, tethered by a translucent chord of life-force or chi[33] suspended and flowing through your body. This energy nexus extends hierarchically upward from the base of your spine, to the top of your scull. Each individual circuit represents a major behavior mode or center of consciousness, from basic survival instinct to extra-sensory perception and beyond. The lower circuits model mundane human behaviors, while the higher circuits model a framework that transcends time and space. It is important to realize that this transcendence of space/time is available to all earthlings at any moment by means of imagination: Before you can realize it, you first must imagine it.

As suggested above, each of the eight circuits may be visualized as corresponding to the "Chakra" system taught by various Hindi schools of thought. Circuit one through seven, line up (approximately) with the seven chakras localized in the earthling body. Circuit one equates to the "Muladhara" or base chakra, and so on. Although each circuit does not correspond exactly with the eastern teachings for each chakra, the analogy is a useful one for locating each of the first seven circuits within the earthling body. Circuit eight is non-local.

---

[33] In traditional Chinese culture, qi (also chi, ch'i or ki) is an active life-force principle forming part of any living thing.

Upon reflection, the notion of the eighth circuit being non-local is quite a phenomenal proposition. The eighth circuit in effect becomes the vehicle of transmission with universe. It is the networked link and the means (matrix) whereby universe and the individual communicate. Individual and universe form a partnership that co-experiences existence. This partnership is communicated through synchronistic means, which from the perspective of the first four circuits, or "normal awareness" seems to defy logic.

This system assumes a biological three-brain nexus, consisting of the brain (itself a bi-lateral system), the heart & the gut. Recent[34] science indicates the human heart and stomach contain nerve cells or neurons that produce and emit neurotransmitters. These scientific revelations allow for a more complex understanding of how our nervous system works. We literally use our heart & gut, in addition to our head, to think and feel.

Mirroring this three-brain nexus, each circuit has a three phase cycle of development:

1.) Reception
2.) Integration
3.) Implementation

Reception of stimuli introduces us to new information. Integration allows for incorporation of new stimuli, into our understanding or world-view. Implementation occurs, when we begin to utilize and "act upon" new integrated information. As we will learn, this framework is an invaluable artifact in the pursuit of mastering Tek-Gnostics.

Circuits one through Four - *Temporal Consciousness*

As the earthling baby develops, each circuit generally becomes active in succession. Circuits one through four, are inherent in every earthling and function automatically according to the DNA blueprint. They are "temporal" in the sense that they are consensual to all

---

[34] See the work of Dr. J. Andrew Armour, on Neurocardiology & Michael Gershon, MD: The Second Brain (HarperCollins, 1999).

earthlings and obey the agreed upon laws of physics. Each circuit activates or is activated by a basic stage of development. Circuit one at birth... Circuit two as the toddler begins to walk... Circuit three as the child develops speech... And circuit four at puberty.

Circuit One
Analogy: Infantile, survival brain/mind... imprinted upon the mother.

After the incredible journey of being born, the earthling baby has earned the bliss of cuddling in his/her mother's arms. Automated survival instincts of suckling and clinging to mother's breast activate. This reality is primarily 2-Dimentional, wherein the babe's surroundings are less important beyond being loved, safe and warm.

Circuit Two
Analogy: Toddler, locomotive brain/mind... political brain. 3-D space.

When a toddler gets his/her wheels (learns to walk), he/she becomes a full-fledged member of the clan. Circuit two activates mastery of one's dexterity and the manipulation (both physically and politically) of one's surroundings. The parenting phenomena known as the "terrible twos" is a result of circuit two development.

Circuit Three
Analogy: Child, language/conceptual brain/mind... 4-D time.

As the child masters locomotion and politics, circuit three activates the ability to conceptualize and use tools/artifacts. The most intricate, mind manifesting and powerful artifact is language. The ability to communicate in a sophisticated manner allows access to the clan's available knowledge. Peer group activity becomes the paramount re-enforcement signal. Mastery of the concept of time allows the ability to reflect and predict.

Circuit Four
Analogy: Adolescent... sexual/emotional brain/mind... Heart/Mind.

Circuit four is most often triggered through hormonal activation. These emotion regulating chemicals mutate the body into the adult form. As the earthling body transforms, alarming and dramatic emotional changes occur. Not to worry... these physical and emotional outbursts are actually quite normal. They are necessary exercises in opening the fourth or "Heart" circuit.

Modern scientific understanding of the afore-mentioned three-brain nexus sheds light upon and validates "old wives" notions of heart and gut thinking. Having a "gut reaction" to an emergent event takes on new meaning in this regard. Thinking with one's heart instead of one's head, historically meant that person wasn't being logical... was being too emotional. The three-brain model aligns this form of thinking with something akin to intuition. It likely indicates early use of higher circuit functioning, such as the early and sporadic experience of the phenomena known as... synchronicity.

Crossing the Valley of the Shadow

There exists between the four, lower mundane circuits and the four, higher transcendental circuits, a conceptual chasm of doubt. This moment comes to all who question the meaning of existence, beyond the corporal provision of survival and security needs. The ancient Gnostic mystics called this mental no-man's-land, the: *Valley of the Shadow of Death*. The more literal translation of the archaic text being: Deep Darkness.

The famous and most often quoted 23rd Psalm[35] of the Old Testament, not only commentates on the Valley of the Shadow, it synchronistically ties the balancing point, or no-man's land of the Eight Circuit Model, into the contemporary phenomenon known as the 23 enigma.[36] This phenomenon was popularized by none other than Robert Anton Wilson, as first recognized by William S Burroughs (Note: Beware as you read these words dear reader, as the 23 enigma now virally infests your consciousness, too).

The Valley of the Shadow metaphor refers to a significant crisis of belief wherein an individual is faced with profound questioning of his/her world view. This event begins with the questioning of one's assumptions of the meaning of life, or how the world works. Invariably, this quandary leads to a realization of the inequity of the human condition and/or the shallowness of one's earlier

---

[35] See: https://en.wikipedia.org/wiki/Psalm_23
[36] See: https://en.wikipedia.org/wiki/23_enigma

assumptions. This moment comes as a shock, as we had grown comfortable with our previous world view, thank you very much.

The Valley of the Shadow, or Deep Darkness, is akin to the more modern and intellectually accessible concept of the Dark Night of the Soul. The connotation of Dark Night of the Soul infers a spiritual bankruptcy of the materialism of mundane existence. Again, Leary and RA Wilson, et al, metaphorically referred to this moment of crisis, utilizing the epic "Quest for the Grail" mythologies (such as Chrétien de Troyes' unfinished poem: Perceval), as... Chapel Perilous.

"Chapel Perilous, like the mysterious entity called "I" ...cannot be located in the space/time continuum; it is weightless, odorless, tasteless and undetectable by ordinary instruments. Indeed, like the Ego, it is even possible to deny that it is there. And yet, even more like the Ego, once you are inside it, there doesn't seem to be any way to ever get out again, until you suddenly discover that it has been brought into existence by thought and does not exist outside thought. Everything you fear is waiting with slavering jaws in Chapel Perilous, but if you are armed with the wand of intuition, the cup of sympathy, the sword of reason, and the pentacle of valor, you will find there (the legends say) the Medicine of Metals, the Elixir of Life, the Philosopher's Stone, True Wisdom and Perfect Happiness."

- Robert Anton Wilson

Circuits Five through Eight - Meta Consciousness

As the earthling enters adulthood, the potential for the activation of circuits five through eight become available. These circuits are of an increasingly transcendental nature. Where circuit one through four are said to be analytical in nature, circuits five through eight are intuitive and psychedelic in nature.

The activation of the higher circuits, are analogous to the development of the extra-ordinary human capabilities alluded to in chapter one. Activation of the higher circuits triggers the evolutionary next-step... the crossing of the human-singularity threshold. Again, from the first chapter... what has been labeled paranormal... is not out of our reach, it is rather, our inheritance.

Circuit Five
Analogy: Ecstatic Brain/mind... Imprinted by peak experiences. Non-ordinary

reality or being "High."

Circuit five is activated by repeated and consistent application of various highly sophisticated technologies developed by ancient earthling initiates. These practices take many forms to appeal to a wide audience. Athletics, drama, literature and music are a few examples of such technologies, as well as the traditional practice of meditation. As an earthling excels in any of these yogas, they achieve a state of concentration and skill that produces an ecstatic or euphoric sensation within the body/mind. The resulting elevated sense of well being and comprehension (being high) insures repeated practice.

Circuit Six
Analogy: Meta-programming brain/mind. Thinking about thinking... Re-programming old imprints... Reality Selection.

Circuit six is associated with so called psi phenomena such as pre-cognition and telepathic ability. Modern physics describes all matter as vibratory in nature. Hence, in interpersonal communication, the implementation of circuit six is perceived by earthlings as "picking up on the vibes" of another individual.

The implementation phase of circuit six may be thought of as creative reality selection or the afore-mentioned meta-programming as described by Dr. John C. Lilly, M.D. in his book: *Programming and Metaprogramming in the Human Biocomputer.* The ability to redesign one's reality is known as the Art of Magick in certain circles (pun intended). The basic concept is that if one has focus and technique, one can re-define the way one sees and interacts with universe.

Circuit Seven
Analogy: Collective unconscious brain/mind... Species wisdom retrieval.

Here is where we tap into the earthling collective... past, present and future. Circuit seven is the collective unconscious mind/brain of Dr. Carl Jung. It is believed by science that all of humanity's evolutionary history is archived within the double helix of our DNA. This information may be accessed via activation of circuit seven. The nineteenth century esoteric school, known as Theosophy, refers to a vast etheric archive of humanity, located in the astral plane of existence. This astral archive is known as the Akashic Records. This mythology can be viewed as another analogy of circuit seven. Accordingly, reincarnation and past life regression may be alternative interpretations of aspects of a fully functional circuit seven.

Returning to the chakra analogy, circuit seven is analogous to the "Sahasrara," or crown chakra... the Thousand Petal Lotus Flower. This energy vortex is the highest circuit within the earthling body. This circuit is in direct communication with universe, which is visualized as an eighth circuit elevated above the earthling's head.

Circuit Eight
Analogy: Galactic brain/mind... Non local access to universal matrix.

Contact. The ability for earthlings to be in communication with non-local (other worldly) intelligence has been recorded since the dawn of time. Out of body experience, cosmic consciousness, communion... there are many interpretations. One of the greatest and least offensive verbs used to describe these phenomena is: *inspiration*. To be inspired is arguably the very basis for all human creativity and cultural development.

It is important to note that although the eight circuits are described above as being activated sequentially, any or all circuits may be activated at any time. As in the description of the N8P, each circuit may also be perceived as a single facet within the whole system. Each earthling is unique, as is each earthling's life experiences. Anything can happen. Trauma, sever physical exertion, as well as natural tendencies may spontaneously trigger any circuit... at any time.

Taken as individual facets of a single gem, the eight circuits of consciousness are a shining example of the conceptual artifacts utilized within intelligence engineering.

The Way to Virtuous Power

During the development of our intelligence engineering systems, certain synergies, certain commonalities in structure began to emerge. Seemingly divergent disciplines such as philosophy, mathematics and music demonstrated similarity in descriptive organization. The overarching synchronistic principle that arose, as if of its own accord, is what we term the: "Law of Eights."

A most profound example of the Law of Eights can be found in the ancient oriental divination system known as the "I-Ching" or "Book of Changes." At first glance, the I-Ching is simply a book of divination. However, upon scrutiny, deeper, timeless connotations emerge. The text of the I-Ching consists of 64 glyphs or "hexagrams" composed of six stacked lines (configured in two trigrams), either solid or broken, which serve as a binary code system. Each hexagram is accompanied by a concise oracular statement or commentary. This commentary essentially interprets the exact moment in time, wherein the hexagram was generated.

Early methodology of identifying a glyph was known as casting. Originally, casting was performed using dried and prepared yarrow stalks. The stalks were cast upon the ground and then interpreted. Later, the yarrow stalks were replaced by the casting of three coins. When cast, each coin would generate either a 0 or a 1 (heads or tails). This binary code continues to be a widely used system of decision making, outside of the I-Ching process. As such, flipping a coin… heads or tail… is perhaps the most universal mechanism of synchronicity… in use today.

It is believed that the I-Ching originated with the mythical ruler of ancient China, Fu Xi. Legends indicate that Fu Xi had the original 8 trigrams (bagua) revealed to him on the shell of a tortoise. By some accounts, the trigrams were revealed on the back of a mythic dragon horse. Over time, the eight trigrams were expanded into the 64 (8x8) hexagram system. Not surprisingly, Carl Jung recognized the I-Ching as a mechanism or artifact of synchronicity…

"Whoever invented the I-Ching, was convinced that the hexagram worked out in a certain moment coincided with the latter in quality no less than in time. To him the hexagram was the exponent of the moment in which it was cast …inasmuch as the hexagram was understood to be an indicator of the essential situation prevailing in the moment of its origin.

This assumption involves a certain curious principle that I have termed synchronicity, a concept that formulates a point of view diametrically opposed to that of (Western) causality. Synchronicity takes the coincidence of events in space and time as meaning something more than mere chance, namely, a peculiar interdependence of objective events among themselves as well as with the subjective (psychic) states of the observer or observers.

The ancient Chinese mind contemplates the cosmos in a way comparable to that of the modern physicist, who cannot deny that his model of the world is a decidedly psycho-physical structure."

- Carl Jung

Jung clearly saw that the ancient oracular system acted as a quantifying mechanism, identifying meaningful coincidence... or in his words... synchronicity. In this way, the I-Ching maps out (interprets) the meaningful connection between an individual's intention and that intention's exact moment in space/time. This moment exerts influence, not only over the past, but into the future. So it is that the ancient divination tool, serves also as an identifier mechanism of synchronicity.

Along with the appropriated wisdom of the Buddha and the oracular structure of the I-Ching, the Tek-Gnostics system is informed by another great intelligence engineer, one: Lao Tzu. It is not historically clear that Lao Tzu was in fact, a single individual. It may be that the remarkably succinct book attributed to Lao Tzu: the *Tao Te Ching*, was a compilation of the prehistoric wisdom of the "Ancient Ones." One cannot help but be reminded of the global mythologies surrounding the ancient ones (also implied as ultra-terrestrials in chapter five) Indeed, the ancient ones, also called ancient masters, are referred to repeatedly within the text.

"Tao" literally means "way", but was extended to mean "The Way." This term, which was variously used by other Chinese philosophers, has special meaning within the context of Taoism, where it implies the essential, unnamable process of universe. "Te" means: "virtue", "personal character," "inner strength" (virtuosity), or "integrity." The semantics of this Chinese word resemble English virtue, which developed from virtù, a now-archaic sense of "inner potency" or "divine power" to the modern meaning of "moral excellence" or "goodness." "Ching" as it is used here means "canon," "great book," or "classic." Thus, Tao Te Ching can be translated as "The Classic/Canon of the Way/Path to Virtuous Power.

Taken together, the *Tao Te Ching, I-Ching* the and the *Eight Circuit model of Consciousness*, as articulated by Leary, et al... build upon the foundation of the noble eight-fold path... to move the organic system that is the law of eights, into the 21st century. These are not static, irrelevant philosophic relics of the past. They are vibrant, living systems that have survived the ravages of time, bringing new insight to contemporary existence.

There are many oracular tools that can achieve synchronistic results. However the nature of the 8x8 or 64 grid that is the I-Ching, functions in synergy with the eight circuit model within the Tek-Gnostics system. Like the myriad other eight-based systems, such as the octave musical scale, the classic 64 square chess board and even the DNA genetic code, the I Ching aligns in the eight-fold format. Thus does the "law of eights" permeate human philosophic history, as well as inform modern science.

And lest we forget… the number 8 is infinity spelled sideways!

So it is that the new Law of Eights, mutate and expand, perhaps exponentially, into our shared future. Just as the Buddha rediscovered the noble eight-fold path, so do we rediscover, add to, and pass along these profound tools of consciousness to the next generation. Who knows what form the ancient law of eights will take… the next time around...

11
THE EIGHT-FOLD PATH RELOADED

"When the best student hears about Tek-Gnostics,
he practices it assiduously.
When the average student hears about Tek-Gnostics,
it seems to him one moment there
and gone the next.
When the worst student hears about Tek-Gnostics,
he laughs out loud.
If he did not laugh... It would be unworthy of being
Tek-Gnostics!"

- from the Tek-Gnostics Codex

We live in a strange world... getting stranger by the nanosecond. Sever environmental stress caused in part by over-harvesting of natural resources... increasing indications of approaching worldwide climate change... global economic collapse on a scale never before dreamed imaginable... overt and covert military-terrorist actions, sanctioned by the very governmental agencies that were created to keep the peace... the list goes on and on. With the abundant wealth our planet has to offer, continually compromised by human mismanagement ...it's a wonder that we're still collectively here at all. With that said, the proverbial "seed of opportunity" resides deep within current dangers...

Life in the information age requires the modern earthling to make increasingly complex decisions with an increased sense of urgency. Given the immediacy in which we must respond... the potential for miscalculation increases exponentially. The consequence of this quickening necessitates the need for strategic adaptation on the part of each of us. Given this immediacy, the following questions arise: Can the individual Intelligence Engineer live a life of integrity and make a difference in his/her world? Is there a course of right action or code of conduct that will aid him/her along their path?

The author of this book does not have exacting insight or otherwise claim to have a better fix on the dilemma surrounding the current human condition. However, ways and means exist to improve upon our situation. Intelligence Engineering systems can be put into play. As indicated in the last chapter, the Tek-Gnostics iE system has been aggregated from a myriad of time-honored academic, philosophic and spiritual paths. No turn has been left un-stoned in its conception!

Again, the eight-fold philosophic structure can be found in many of humanity's most ancient teachings, as well as in modern science. In modern physics for example, the Eightfold Way is a term coined by American physicist Murray Gell-Mann[37] for a theory organizing subatomic baryons and mesons into octets. As indicated earlier, the Buddhist Noble Eight-fold path stands out as a particularly profound archaic example.

So it is that the techniques of awakened action that inform Tek-Gnostics align with the archaic Law of Eights principle. Within the manifesto illustrated below, our version of the law of eights include a three-phase approach of implementation.

In its comprehension, the Tek-Gnostics three fold approach cycles from reception and integration, into implementation. In its utilization, our reactions take the form of a three phase approach of awakened action: peace, pleasure and passion. This three-fold model of awakened action was inspired by the works of Ekhart Tolle.[38] If consistently implemented, each of us can effectively alter the vibrational frequency of our consciousness.

---

[37] See: https://en.wikipedia.org/wiki/Murray_Gell-Mann
[38] See: https://en.wikipedia.org/wiki/Eckhart_Tolle

The Tek-Gnostics Eight-Fold Path
A Manifesto of "Vigilant Consciousness" in the 21st Century.

The first step in our journey toward a mind/body centered neural autonomy is an issuance of the following *Eight-Fold Tek-Gnostics Manifesto,* consisting of an octet of concise tenets. These eight tenets serve as a streamlined "rules of the road" for the modern intelligence engineer. In imitation of the noble eight-fold path of Buddhism and the octagonal trigrams of the Taoist bagua, it is with a deceptive simplicity that we present our manifesto in the familiar form of the ancient Law of Eights. As we shall see... this consciousness hacking conceptual artifact, a combination of mindfulness, humor, acceptance of the moment, and creativity... will prove to be a powerful cornerstone within the iE system of Tek-Gnostics...

Tenets one through four:

1.) Wake up!
Think for yourself! The single most important factor in decision making is to be cognizant. Being conscious and mentally agile will allow that light bulb that appears over your head to blink on more often. Be smart... Incorporate the concept of Intelligence Engineering into your daily life. Be mindful... know that the present moment is the filament of infinity. How can you drive down the highway of right action if you're asleep at the wheel?

2.) Turn on your Lovelight!
Of equal importance as item one... In everything we think, say or do, we must come from the heart. Advancements in Neurocardiology confirm the existence of neurons in the human heart, as well as a networked interface with the gut & brain. Temper your thoughts with feeling so as to balance your perceptions. As part of your nervous system, your heart is the mechanism by which you apply intuitive discernment. Trust your heart (and gut) to guide you through life's ambiguities. When making decisions, do you listen to that calm, quiet voice within?

3.) Leave it on!
Consistency in heart-felt action is key... Once you get to a

balanced head/heart/gut state of consciousness, the idea is to stay there as much as possible. Once you feel the groove, use your head and stay with it! Remember, the heart isn't wishy washy... and it is always right! A balance of head, heart and gut will allow you to be in the "eternal now" more frequently. How often during the day are you in the eternal now?

4.) Do unto others.

The Buddha claimed that compassion is the highest form of human emotion. Compassion here is defined as a marriage of concepts one & two... using your intellect, feeling with your heart and following your gut, to formulate a "Right Thinking" and "Right Action." Think for yourself in order to discern all the options, trust your heart in order to make compassionate choices and follow your gut instincts. The golden rule applies here... "Do unto others as you would have them do unto you" ...When interacting with others, do you see a separate being, or a mirror?

Note: The understanding and incorporation of the fourth tenet of our Eight-Fold Path, also acts as a departure point between the lower four or primary tenets... and the higher four or secondary tenets. Before moving on, let us place our attention for a moment upon the rule of reciprocity, as well as the three mind-sets arising from such.

The Golden Rule

Also known as the ethic of reciprocity, the Golden Rule is perhaps humanity's oldest global ethical code of conduct. It is arguably the most essential basis for the modern concept of human rights, in which each individual has a right to just treatment and a responsibility to ensure justice for others. A key element of the Golden Rule is that a person attempting to live by this rule treats all people, not just members of his or her tribe, with the same consideration he or she would want to be shown, by others.

In the daily incorporation of the golden rule, there are three appropriate mind-sets arising from this code... from which the Intelligence Engineer proceeds. The three mind-sets (the 3 P's) of awakened action or what we refer to as following the tekgnostic path are: peace, pleasure and passion. Constant vigilance is required to insure that the actions of the intelligence engineer emanate from one of these three mind-sets, for they align with the creative power of universe.

Peace - This modality arises from the realization that not all experiences are enjoyable. At times, one must accept certain unfortunate circumstances... be at peace with them and respond with surrendered action. Performing an action in a state of peace... being patient, tolerant... means you non-judgmentally accept the situation, while you deal with it. This mind-set is known in Eastern Schools of thought as: Karma Yoga. Chop wood... carry water. The afore-mentioned peace is a subtle energy vibration which then flows into what you do. And that subtle energy vibration... is consciousness.

Pleasure - The peace that comes with surrendered action turns to a sense of aliveness when you actually enjoy what you are doing. This pleasure is the dynamic aspect of being. When the creative power of universe becomes conscious of itself, it manifests as pleasure or enjoyment. Pleasure does not come from what you do, it flows into what you do and thus into this world from deep within you. When you enjoy doing something, you are really experiencing the joy of Universal Being in its dynamic aspect. That's why anything you find pleasure in doing, connects you with the power behind all creation.

Passion - This modality is expressed as a deep, profound pleasure in what you do... plus the added element of a creative goal or a vision that you work toward. When you add a goal to the pleasure of what you do, the energy field or vibrational frequency changes. At the height of creative activity, fueled by enthusiastic passion, there will be enormous intensity and energy behind what you do. Again, this is the passion of the *Amateur*. Sustained passion brings into existence a wave of creative energy. All you have to do then, in the surfer parlance... is "catch the wave"*!*

If we do not proceed from a place of peace, pleasure or passion within our daily activities... it is advisable that we discontinue the activity immediately. Otherwise, we are not taking responsibility for our state of consciousness. Responsibility for our personal consciousness is the single most important facet of our earthly existence. If we do not take responsibility for our state of consciousness, we are not taking responsibility for our life. Moving on...

Tenets five through eight:

5.) Nothing is so sacred that it cannot be made fun of.

A well developed sense of humor is indicative of a well developed intellect. Have fun with this. If you are having fun in your endeavors, then chances are you are learning. If you quit having fun, you quit learning. If you quit learning, then you will be visited by that most dreaded and humorless specter: boredom. Every school child knows how intolerable boredom is. Are we having fun yet?

6.) The circumstances are necessarily perfect.

"All is chaos under Heaven and the situation is excellent!!!" (Chairman Mao). Be mindful of the situation. Chaotic events in life arise. Shit happens. In life, there are some variables that are within our power to control and others that are not. The myriad of variables associated with specific events are not always easily discernible. Be open to the possibility that events, whether good or ill, may come about in some measure independent of your trajectory. Often, when confronted with a situation, how we perceive and react to the situation will dramatically alter the outcome. Is the cup half full?

7.) Dare to be naïve!

This famous quote from the high tekgnostic adept: R. Buckminster Fuller is apropos. Our outlook toward life and the inevitable emergent situations we confront is the determining factor in how we proceed. Cynicism can be a cruel master. If we fall into the bad mental habits of gloom, doom & disdain, we will surely bring those attitudes about. Beware negative vibrations! Be like two fried eggs and keep your sunny side up! Is it disquieting to be perceived as naïve?

8.) We're all Bozos on this Bus.

We're all in this together. There is no "them" ...it's only us. No one is really any cooler or smarter or holier than anyone else. The best and easiest way for us all to make it (wherever that is!) is to help each other. Lend a hand. If you see someone struggling with partial awareness, help them if you can. Wit and humor are our ammunition in this enterprise. A good, well timed delivery is our weapon. Can you launch a humor bomb without hurting anybody's feelings?

Note: In case you didn't notice, the preceding eight-fold path is also a pop quiz. It serves the double-duty of being an entrance exam for those among you who wish to pursue the "Inner Mysteries" of Tek-Gnostics. Each individual item poses at least one question. The way in which we answer each question is indicative of how we will fare in our exploration of universe.

Additionally, within the Tek-Gnostics three-fold path or mind-set of awakened action, there are three distinct levels, (degrees) from which each tekgnostic practitioner perceives and interacts with his or her world. Before finishing this chapter, please re-read the quote from the Tek-Gnostics codex, found at the beginning of the chapter.

Our first challenge is to discover from which level of perception each of us issues, in our worldly interactions. Are we the best of students? Do we practice diligently? Are we average students? Is our practice here one moment and gone the next? Do we laugh out loud?

We need to contemplate our strategies and carry them out with "panache" and style. Inventiveness and a healthy sense of humor (itself a sure indicator of intelligence), will be our modus operandi. Compassion and humility will act as our compass. The company and interaction of like-minded individuals will be our point of reference. Together, the artifacts of the Law of Eights combine to assist us in our navigation through this strange and wonderful world in which we live.

The above manifesto is just a beginning. The ideas that are presented here are simple ones ...So simple as to be overlooked most of the time. But being mindful is the essential point... is it not? If, in the course of our travels, we keep these eight concepts in mind, they may help to illuminate the otherwise dimly lit path that traverses our experience of the human condition...

12
THE TEK-GNOSTIC PATH

"Rid yourself of desire... in order to realize Universal mystery.
Allow yourself to have desire...
in order to experience Universal manifestation.
These two are essentially the same, but diverge in the naming.
Mystery upon Mystery... the gateway to tekgnosis."

- from the Tek-Gnostics Codex

Having outlined the historic pedigree and the eight-fold structure of Tek-Gnostics... we can now delve a little deeper into the essential nature of our synchronistic awareness artifact...

Tek-Gnostics is a conceptual chameleon. It is at once a mythology, a revival of the ancient mysteries, a science fiction, a philosophic system and an aggregated esoteric information hub. It aggregates those earthling artifacts, technologies and bodies of knowledge that facilitate human consciousness and its interaction with universe. It is an outpost on the frontier of Earth's info-sphere... an oasis in the desert of post-industrial, post-religious modernity. Tek-Gnostics' technologies arise from the premise that the best way to understand universe and our place in it, is through direct experience and knowledge or "Gnosis."

Tek-Gnostics serves a wide array of functions, depending upon how it is perceived and referenced by its user. The "experiencer" or practitioner of this system is referred to as a: *tekgnostic*. The singular revelatory experience of our artifact-assisted gnosis... that ah-ha moment, as augmented using our tek, we call: *tekgnosis*. The systematic pursuit, codification and application of these experiences, the structure or "school of thought" ...we label: *Tek-Gnostics*.

The tekgnostic path is self-verifying in the sense that it unfolds within as it unfolds without. This is the fundamental tekgnostic relationship: observer and observed... spirit and universe... self and matrix. The genesis of infinite universe, or that which cannot be named, is perfect. The fabric of our universe or Matrix, as it is referred to within the Tek-Gnostics codex, is necessarily perfect. This qualifier exemplifies the essential Gnostic principle that the dualistic, materialistic universe we live in... is not perfect.

More importantly, the "powers that be" which are instrumental in shaping our world are far from perfect. This is an essential theme in traditional Gnostic thought. "The gods must be crazy." In their cosmology, the various Gnostic sects shared a common mythic allegory that the universe was created by a deranged creator demigod. Before delving deeper into the tekgnostic path, a short primer on traditional Gnosticism is in order...

Gnosticism (from Ancient Greek: γνωστικός gnostikos, "learned," from γνῶσις gnōsis, knowledge) is a contemporary term used to describe a specific grouping of ancient mystery schools and/or religious orders' cosmological understandings. Most of what we know today about Gnosticism was uncovered in the waning years of World War II, in a collection of papyrus codices, known as the Nag Hammadi library. This collection of Gnostic texts was discovered near the Upper Egyptian town of Nag Hammadi, by a local farmer named Muhammed al-Samman, in 1945.

The discovery of the Nag Hammadi Library (and the Dead Sea Scrolls... see below) took place within 2 years of Dr Hoffman's legendary synthesis of the Ergot fungus, *Claviceps purpurea*. Once again, for the purposes of this narrative, it goes far beyond coincidence that these two mysteriously synchronous events... the discovery of ancient Gnostic texts and the discovery of LSD-25, would both occur virtually at the same time. This connection will be made clear later.

The writings in these discovered codices consist of fifty-two Gnostic essays. They also included three works belonging to the *Corpus Hermeticum*[39] and a partial translation/reinterpretation of Plato's *Republic*.[40] Prior to the discovery of the Nag Hammadi Library, much of what we knew about Gnosticism was preserved only in the condemnations of Gnosticism, by early church fathers. In his work on the Nag Hammadi Library, Professor Emeritus of Religion, James Robinson suggested that these discovered codices possibly (originally) belonged to a nearby Pachomian[41] monastery, and were buried after the Council of Nicaea's condemnation of the use of non-canonical scripture.

The other widely cited, post-WWII archaeological (and synchronistic) discovery pertaining to Gnosticism, is known as the Dead Sea Scrolls. A collection of some 981 different texts discovered between 1946 and 1956, the Dead Sea Scrolls were discovered near the Dead Sea in the Palestinian West Bank, in the immediate vicinity of the ancient settlement at Khirbet Qumran. These scrolls have traditionally been identified with an ancient mystical sect known as the Essenes.[42] Certain scholars maintain that the Gnostic traditions descended from this earlier sect.

The Gnostic and Essene traditions shared similar mystic, eschatological, messianic, and ascetic beliefs. Theodor H. Gaster, in his work: *The Dead Sea Scriptures in English Translation* (1956) indicated that the Scrolls are essentially mystical documents and that the experiences spoken of in the document called the "Scroll of Hymns" are genuine mystical experiences...

The "wondrous mysteries" of God revealed to the authors of the Scrolls according to their testimony remind one of similar mysteries and mystical experiences alluded to and documented in various Gnostic scriptures, notably the Nag Hammadi collection. This is another similarity connecting the Essenes with the later Gnostic Christians, since we find such similarities in their religious theologies.

It is more than likely that the Essenic authors of the Scrolls, not unlike the Gnostic authors of the Nag Hammadi codices, were partakers of visions and

---

[39] See: https://en.wikipedia.org/wiki/Hermetica
[40] See: https://en.wikipedia.org/wiki/The_Republic_(Plato)
[41] See: https://en.wikipedia.org/wiki/Pachomius_the_Great
[42] See: https://en.wikipedia.org/wiki/Essenes

revelations of an esoteric nature and that the content of the Scrolls could be viewed as possessing an inner, hidden meaning or code. The Essenes were in fact inclined to employ codes, as the discovery of the so-called Taxo-Asaph disguise by way of the use of the Atbash cipher proves."

- Theodor H. Gaster

In turn, some scholars suggest a connection between Gnosticism and Buddhism. An early suggestion of the connection of Gnostic teachings with Buddhism was put forth by the Saint Petersburg Tibetologist, Isaac Jacob Schmidt. This was further developed by Edward Conze in his paper: *Buddhism and Gnosis* presented to the Origins of Gnosticism: colloquium of Messina, held on the 13th, through the 18th of April, 1966.

This congress was a pivotal event in modern revision of scholarship on Gnosis and Gnosticism in Judaism and early Christianity. Conze considered Mahayana Buddhism to be contemporary with the origins of Christianity. Conze noted that:

"This Buddhism I propose to compare with 'Gnosis' rather than the Gnostics, because the connotation of the latter term is still so uncertain."

Conze's suggestion were supported and expanded by Elaine Pagels in: *The Gnostic Gospels* (New York, 1979).

Still other scholars suggest the connection between Gnosticism and Hinduism. For example... both Hinduism and Gnosticism preach a universal Godhead, an absolute Divine that is unknowable but toward which we must all strive to rejoin... called "Brahman" by the Hindu's and the "Pleroma" by the Gnostics. A demiurge created the world we live in, which is illusory. This demiurge is the god "Maya" in Hinduism, which is also the name of the world of illusion in which we live. It is named "Ialdabaoth" (Yaldabaoth) by the Gnositics... the imperfect God of the Old Testament. The Hindi Brahman and the Gnostic Pleroma both exist beyond the veils of this false word.

Apparently, Gnostic ideas are found in many ancient religions that teach that humanity is "not of this Earth." Those who we refer to as Gnostics, viewed the material world as suspect. They saw themselves as strangers in a strange land... divine beings, trapped in earthly bodies. Again, their cosmology included a supreme monadic divinity, known as "Pleroma" …an imperfect creator god or demiurge, which is an illusion… an emanation from the single monad or source… and a doctrine of salvation in which the divine (human) element may be returned to the divine realm through a process of awakening, or Gnosis.

In Gnosticism, the world of the demiurge is represented by the lower world, which is associated with matter, flesh, time and more particularly… an imperfect, ephemeral world. The world of God is represented by the upper world and is associated with the soul and perfection. The world of God is eternal and not part of the physical. It is intangible, shadowy and timeless. Gnosis (esoteric or intuitive knowledge) is the way to salvation of the soul from the material world.

You're either on the Path, or you're off the Path

We will explore other concepts of traditional Gnosticism in greater detail, momentarily. For now, suffice it to say that the intention of the study of our contemporary Tek-Gnostics is to provide a system of understanding in which self-verification of perceived reality is an underlying component. The true, definitive intent… the spirit in which Tek-Gnostics is presented… is to provide a framework and a network for consciousness exploration and epiphany.

This pursuit is not for everyone, however. The exploration of consciousness requires a certain intrepid curiosity. It is not for the faint of heart, for it requires a brutally honest self assessment. As epitomized by medieval alchemists, one must be prepared to enter into the "Great Work" …the work upon oneself, unwaveringly. Walking the tekgnostic path… the path less travelled… requires discipline, resiliency and resourcefulness. This is a commitment that most choose not to make, for the pathway to tekgnosis is as narrow and as difficult to walk upon as the proverbial razor's edge.

Any intrepid tekgnostic embarking upon this journey of discovery must know that at some point along the path, he or she will face, and must pass through the Deep Darkness… the Valley of the Shadow, as typified in chapter ten.

Entering into this "great work" can be perceived as existential[43] in

---

[43] See: https://en.wikipedia.org/wiki/Existentialism

nature. To work upon oneself can be a lonely endeavor. It involves questioning one's assumptions on the very nature of reality. There comes with this work, however, a redemptive certainty of one's relationship with universe. Individual and universe form the partnership that co-experience human existence. The practice of this partnership is communicated through synchronistic means, relying on certain mythic commonalities.

From the essential perspective of synchronistic a-causality... there is no difference between individual and universe. All is one, in balance with that which cannot be named. These two entities are the same, but diverge in "the naming" as they issue forth into existence. This manifest relational aspect is foundational within Tek-Gnostics. The role of the individual is to bear witness... to experience the miracle and wonder that is material, universal existence.

From the perspective of the material plane of existence, it appears that everything from galaxies... to the individual... to sub-atomic particles is contained within universe. This is communicated in the parlance of the Hermetic tradition with the succinct phrase: "as above, so below." The mythology is here indicating that the structure of universe, as a macrocosm, is similar to the structure of the human body, as a microcosm... the workings of the solar system are likened to the workings of the molecule... wheels within wheels.

Applied Tek-Gnostics

The extent of the effectiveness of this partnership, is dependent upon, revolves around... the epiphanous comprehension of the interplay between essence and application... light and dark... yin and yang... the excited (active) state vs the resting (passive) state of existence. For it is precisely in the reception and contemplation of miracle and wonder that new information is revealed to us. New information, when incorporated into our understanding or world view becomes... intelligence.

At this epiphanous moment, the individual's incorporation or processing of intelligence (intel) or new information may take one of two forms. The first: overt, active, applicative form... is where the tekgnostic practitioner, upon reaching a calm centered state, consciously contemplates the new information. Here one processes the new information by actively thinking about it... pondering... looking at the new intel from as many perspectives... as many angles...

as possible. Simply put, this applicative form of contemplation can be considered our Tek.

The second: covert, passive, essential form... wherein the tekgnostic, upon reaching a calm centered state, clears his or her mind of all thought, allowing the processing of new information to be of an unconscious nature. Devoid of conscious thought, the new intel is incorporated in the unconscious mind. In this way, the tekgnostic allows the new information to percolate within. Here the contemplation is deeper... akin to the Taoist "Wu Wei" (無爲) ...action through non-action or non-doing. This essential form of contemplation is our Gnosis.

Active acquisition of intel equates to a technology, while passive reception of intel equates to an epiphany.

As a consciousness meta-programming artifact, the myriad data-streams collectively known as "Tek-Gnostics" serve as a suite of tools of inner exploration... as a psychedelic reality modifier. The applied aspect of Tek-Gnostics system is within itself... two-fold in nature. It is a "Yoga," or personal practice, whereby the individual explores the human/consciousness interface. It is also a "Tantra," or system of intelligence increase and communication, taught and shared by the community.

Tek-Gnostics, as a practice, explores and facilitates the concept of "consciousness hacking," in symmetry with intelligence amplification. Originally, the term hacker referred to an enthusiast who tinkered with any kind of system, mechanical or electrical, in order to better-understand how it worked. Today, hackers are persons who create or modify computer software, typically with the goal of using software in a manner not intended by the original computer programmer.

So too it was with the ancient Gnostics, who communed with the divine in a manner not intended by the material world's celestial programmer... ie: the Demiurge.

As we have identified above, Tek-Gnostics is a system. It is a body of work that has been aggregated from a variety of sources, both contemporary and ancient. It is a curriculum of study or Tantra, designed to facilitate individuated gnosis. As such, it becomes exponentially more powerful within a group format. A communally driven system allows for a sharing of information and perspective.

The individual intelligence engineer or "tekgnostic" within a group or cohort... draws upon the experience of the collective.

In this age of social media, we need not look far to see phenomenal examples of such collectives. Social media allows for community, regardless of proximity. Per Marshall McLuhan's vision, the village has indeed become global.

The mass utilization of a globally networked social media application is a real-world example of networked or "Intelligence Amplified Singularity." As Vernor Vinge indicated... global computer networks and their associated users are beginning to "wake up" as a superhumanly intelligent entity. The networked, IA path has not only begun, it is fast becoming well established. Increased computing power, coupled with increasingly more sophisticated social media applications, suggest incredible IA possibilities.

Admittedly, posting pictures of cute lil kitties with bad grammar on Facebook is not a shining example of intelligence amplification. But as the exponentially expanding complexity of our global network grows... as individual users find more sophisticated and creative ways to interact with said networks and each other... IA Singularity approaches.

The modern tekgnostic uses the IA artifact as a medium of choice. For it is in the networked, IA path that humanity can infuse the "human equation" of "soul" and "spirit" within the singularity awakening. Returning to the Tek-Gnostics analogy... the emerging globally awakening computer network is a tool, an artifact. It is the mechanical brain, the AI or Artificial Intelligence. It is our Tek. Humanity's awakened participation within the singularity event is "Natural Intelligence" or knowledge. It is our Gnosis. The synergistic interplay, the balancing of the two, is Tek-Gnostics... or the Intelligence Amplified path to singularity.

Strange things are afoot on Hwy 61

"God said to Abraham, "kill me a son..."

-from "Hwy 61 Revisited" by Bob Dylan

As indicated earlier, Tekgnosticism relies upon intellectual and spiritual experience... a balance of the heart, mind and gut. As the renowned contemporary Gnostic Bishop, Stephan A. Hoeller[44] has so eloquently articulated:

"Gnosis pertains to a specific illuminative understanding that expresses itself best through the medium of mythology. The truths embodied in these myths are of a more personal nature than the dogmas of theology or the statements of philosophy. In this way, the myth acts as a parable or metaphor, illustrating through the actions of the myth, complex insights."

To illustrate this principal, let us examine the ancient Gnostic mythology surrounding the "Demiurge" entity.

Within certain Gnostic schools of thought, there exists a complex of mythologies indicating that the God of the Old Testament, the burning bush God... the God of Abraham... was in fact a lesser entity known to them as the Demiurge. The Demiurge was a delusional "creator" deity. Although subordinate to the all-pervasive Monad or Godhead (what is referred within Tek-Gnostics as... *That which shall remain nameless*), the demiurge believed himself to be the one true God (ie: *"You shall have no other gods before Me"* - Exodus 20:3).

Consequently, within these Gnostic mythologies, the Demiurge proceeded to create the material world, thinking that his creations were the totality of all that is. In his delusion, the Demiurge was blind to the realization of the highest, absolute and unknowable God. To certain ancient Gnostic sects, this delusion was interpreted as "derangement" and the Demiurge was deemed insane. Accordingly, this insanity took the form of confusion, jealousy and malevolence... thus was evil visited upon the world.

Further, the Gnostics held the belief that humanity was not only innocent of the corrupt nature of the world... not only free of original sin... they held within them, a divine spark of the true, transcendent, unknowable Godhead. The corruption that had crept into the material world was rather a product of the Demiurge's derangement. Thus humanity's "original sin" was a fallacy imposed by the early church, propagated with questionable intent.

Considering the Gnostic assertion that the creator God, known in the Old Testament as Yahweh or Jehovah, was indeed insane... this

---

[44] (Born Nov 27, 1931) Hoeller is a scholar of Gnosticism and Jungian psychology, and Regionary Bishop of Ecclesia Gnostica, and the senior holder of the English Gnostic transmission in America.

premise would seem to answer a lot of questions pertaining to the horrific maladies of "being of this world" or life on Earth as we experience it daily. A God that is insane would make "cynical sense" as to all the pain and suffering visited upon the world. In light of this mythology, it would then not seem so horrifically absurd that an insane God would ask Abraham, the founder of all three "Desert Religions" ...to kill his begotten son Isaac, to prove his faith.

It is this enigmatic Gnostic mythology and other variations of it that caused the developing Church bureaucracy of the first century, CE to proclaim that the early Gnostics were indeed heretics. Apparently, the early church fathers did not take kindly to the Gnostic premise that their God of Gods, Yahweh... was an insane, bureaucratic, middle-management God. Again, mythologies such as these, act as parable or metaphor, illustrating through the actions of the myth, complex insights.

The great mythologies of the past often display commonalities, although expressed differently, across different cultures. Similarly, they tend to repeat themselves over the eons. They re-calibrate... modernize... to fit current cultural understanding. Thus the ancient Gods give way to newer mythologies such as monotheism or science or even alien intelligences, as humanity's view of universe evolves.

Certain contemporary mythologies seem to have devolved back into a dogmatic, eschatological, dumbed-down rendering of archaic end-times prophecy. Specifically, the dominant desert religions were (and are) obsessed with imagery of Armageddon... righteous battles, catastrophe and final judgment. These desert religion's more mystical (and suppressed) factions, such as the Kabbalahists, the Sufis and especially the Gnostics, foretold of an Apocalypse (from the Greek: apokálypsis) which literally translates as a "lifting of the veil" or revelation... a steady increase in light... a change in focus from folly to wisdom.

Contemporary desert religious hierarchies seem to condone a violent, fundamentalist prophetic anticipation of a coming messiah/antichrist apocalyptic showdown. Rather than embrace the mystical view, they support a simplistic, us vs them... saved vs damned... and most importantly, for reasons of controlling the masses... pie in the sky, bye and bye, doctrine. This position clearly indicates that contemporary organized religious institutions are primarily governmental (read: manipulative) as opposed to spiritual, in nature.

The "technological singularity" spin put upon this age old myth... the "Geek Rapture" if you will... similarly prophesizes that at the moment when artificial intelligence surpasses human intelligence, the human era ends. The afore mentioned religious hierarchy's fear-driven connotation leads to the portrayal of the emerging AI/human dichotomy as that of an antichrist/messiah cataclysm. Hence humanity recalibrates the old mythology into more of the same apocalyptic fever. We shall return to this line of reasoning, in the next chapter.

With that said, the question is one of perspective. Do we accept the spoon-fed, militaristic "Apocalypse Now" eschatology, as propagandized by the desert religious hierarchies? Or do we choose to embrace the vision of a steady increase in light... a change in focus from folly to wisdom? The ancient Gnostics, Sufis et al, chose to embrace the "lifting of the veil" mythology.

Tek-Gnostics Mythology

Likewise, Tek-Gnostics chooses a mythological increase of light narrative. We choose the mythology of a psychedelic apocalypse. We choose to experience humanity's latest eschatological boogeyman... Technological Singularity... as a lifting of the veil... a change in focus from folly to wisdom. We choose these mythologies to help inform our world view and to empower our interaction within our world, as an intelligence agent... an Intelligence Engineer.

The great Zen master, Alan Watts, often spoke of an ancient Earthling myth in which the sustaining force of Universe (God as it is oftentimes referred to in the West) manifests all that is within Universe while dreaming. As God dreams... the dream transforms into our cosmos, projecting countless billions of tiny holographic specks of itself, to materialize the physical realm. God assumes the roles of galaxies, stars and planets... the myriad creatures of Universe... and thus becomes completely immersed in strange and wonderful adventures, some of which are terrible and frightening.

Since God is all there is within & without Universe and since there is no "other" in which to play with, God plays a cosmic game of "hide & seek" with itself. Hence these adventures we call life, take the form of a great game or play within God's dream.

In the heat of game-play within our cosmic RPG[45] ...God temporarily forgets its true nature of oneness. This forgetfulness seems to span the entire cycle of Universe. Eventually, God awakens from the many dreams and fantasies and remembers its true identity, the one and eternal Self of the cosmos who is never born and never dies. At this moment, all that is... returns to the source. Thus Universe goes round... now advancing... now receding... for eternity.

This elegant, Gnostic-like mythology puts an interesting twist upon the demiurgic allegory. It is of ancient origin, yet can be used to poetically describe the evolving theories of modern physics, in its speculation on the nature of Universe. This particular modern myth resonates with Tek-Gnostics mythology. The tekgnostic consciously choose a mythology devoid of Deific Derangement.

Instead, the tekgnostic system of perception facilitates a way of experiencing all reality, including the manifest cosmos, as the outcome of creative play by the divine absolute. Our system is designed to help us remember our trials and tribulations as a kind of game or drama which is being acted out by the eternal Self of Universe. We strive to be mindful of, and honor the spark of the divine within each of us. God hides in the roles and personalities of separate entities. We... as the physical manifestation of those entities... seek.

We seek to explore our world in pursuit of gnosis... a knowledge that does not come from mere book learning, but from an inspirational flash of insight. Book learning and study is the preparation... the homework, if you will. Gnosis is the moment when the hard work of study pays off... the spark of epiphany that takes one to a deeper level of understanding. This light-bulb moment is the lifting of the veil, the increase of light that the ancient mystics spoke of. It is also an instance of synchronicity, as put forth by Carl Jung.

The tekgnostic does not distinguish between himself and the world...
The needs of other people are as his own.
He is good to those who are good...
he is also good to those who are not good.
Thereby he increases the good.

---

[45] Acronym for Role Playing Game: a game in which players assume the roles of characters in a fictional setting.

He trusts those who are trustworthy...
he also trusts those who are not trustworthy.
Thereby he increases trustworthiness.
The tekgnostic lives in harmony with universe
and his mind is the world's mind.
So... he nurtures the worlds of others as a mother does her children.

-from the Tek-Gnostics Codex

In the pursuit of our explorations, we will employ the existent networking artifacts at our disposal to advance our knowledge and communicate that information. For it is in the utilization and interaction of earth's global electronic medium that the tekgnostic Intelligence Engineer's unique opportunity for acquiring and disseminating knowledge presents itself. In this way, the intelligence amplified path to singularity becomes a marriage of the electronic medium... the artificial intelligence, with the epiphany of human consciousness, with natural intelligence.

This marriage combines the computational power of AI, with the spiritual power of humanity. It is what keeps humanity in the evolutionary game. The balance of human and machine intelligence is the Intelligence Amplified path forward to the Century of Singularity ...and beyond.

13
PLANETARY MATRIX

"As a boy, I once rolled dice in an empty house...
playing against myself.
I suppose I was afraid. It was twilight, and I forget who won.
I was too young to have known that
the old abandoned house in which I played... was the universe.
I would play for man more fiercely...

if the years would take me back."

- Loren Eiseley

Earth Matrix

The Greek philosopher, Aristotle[46] said that man is by nature a social animal. As social beings, it is inherent within us to communicate. As tool builders, it is also within our nature to create and manipulate artifacts. To date, the world-wide web is arguably one of humanity's most ingenious and ambitious artifacts. It is nothing less than a vast working model of global consciousness. Each human with the means (computer, tablet, mobile, etc.) to connect to the web becomes, in a sense, a single, autonomous neuron in the global mind

---

[46] See: https://en.wikipedia.org/wiki/Aristotle

of Gaia, our home world. Given the incredible creative potential each individual earthling brings to this system, the possibilities for our global consciousness artifact are seemingly infinite.

As this global nerve-net becomes more complex and sophisticated, our evolving technologies have accelerated in their sophistication and complexity. Indeed, our terrestrial and satellite communications network encompasses the Earth in such a way as to be as integral to Earth's functioning as one of her atmospheres. This information network or "infosphere" further deepens humanity's potential within Gaia's sentient life support systems.

The timely emergence of this so-called infosphere, may indicate that it is a natural, organic development of Gaia's nervous system. If Earth's environmental systems act as her autonomic nervous system, perhaps humanity and our artifacts, act as her conscious, somatic nervous system. Perhaps we serve as Gaia's expanding and evolving nerve-net. Regardless, our infosphere appears to be on the brink of exponential expansion again, facilitated by what we have come to call... technological singularity.

If the singularity event is a culminating working model of global consciousness, this model intricately facilitates humanity's evolutionary (paranormal) growth. Like any model, it helps us envision and assists us in transition into an awakened tek/human partnership. The model shows us how a man/machine system will work. Thus humanity and our artifacts evolve in tandem into the "century of singularity" as an amalgam of communicative intelligence.

Indeed, the singularity may be seen as an awakening of our collective communicative abilities. A partnership of artificial intelligence, as achieved through the networked, intelligence augmented path, with an evolving, paranormal humanity, becomes an amazingly powerful intelligence entity. Again, perhaps the timely marriage of man and machine is by design. Perhaps this is all "part of the plan." As our technologies are an integral part of us, so too may what we have termed singularity, become an integral part of Gaia.

If we hypothesize that humanity acts as Gaia's self-reflective faculty... if we act as an organic instrument of self consciousness, it follows that we facilitate Gaia's ability to think about Herself. The human collective, as global consciousness, allows our Mother Earth to pause and reflect... to be self aware. This "Eyes of the World" hypothesis may be expanded, by virtue of the spark of divinity within each human, to suggest that we also act as part of universe's self-reflective spiritual sense organ. Perhaps on a much grander scale, Earth is a sleepy dendrite, about to "wake up" in a back-water corner of what we call the Milky Way Galaxy.

Within this mythology, each of us fulfill a dendritic perceptive and communicative role, for our sentient home world. Gaia, orbiting Sol, our local star, in return fulfills a similar sentient role, as an individual within her community... the Milky Way. Our home galaxy thereby joins the universal intelligence community of galaxies, wherein Universe's ultra-sentient persona, aka: God... pauses and thinks: "what a wondrous existence this universe is!" ...wheels within wheels.

Now, within this body of work, universe is analogous to... can be equated to... information (universe=information). Within this premise, information has a very special meaning: Information equals intelligence, or coherent order. This is as distinguished from noise, which is incoherent chaos. Evolution of consciousness is the gradual emergence of information out of chaos. This is the "lifting of the veil" or steady increase in light... the change in focus from folly to wisdom that the ancient Gnostics spoke of. The continuity in universe is not necessarily mere consciousness... but information... coherence. In this regard, the dualistic nature of universe can be expressed, not merely as light versus darkness, but rather: *coherence versus confusion.*

This mythic hypothesis would place humanity in a more profound role... as an intelligence system of Gaia, which in turn plays a role in a galactic and ultimately universal intelligence network. The mechanism whereby Gaia's humanity-wide system sends signals... communicates... is none other than our old friend, synchronicity. Per Jung's theory, synchronicity is acausal, in that it is affected by meaning, rather that causation. It does not appear to be limited or even effected by either space or time. This synchronistic network of communication is available everywhere and every-when at once... on a cellular level, on a human level, as well as on a galactic level. ...wheels within wheels.

Returning to humanity's planetary rise to prominence over the last 10,000 years... this may turn out to primarily be an evolutionary leap for Gaia... rather than merely a human evolution. Viewing Humanity as a sense organ of planet Earth arguably places our rapid evolution as a component of, or a development of Gaia's evolution. However, the question remains as to what was the catalyst that sparked our species' intelligence increase?

The question brings us back to Terrance McKenna and what has been called his "stoned ape" hypothesis. In his 1993 book: *Food of the Gods: The Search for the Original Tree of Knowledge* (sub-titled: *A Radical History of Plants, Drugs, and Human Evolution*), McKenna proposed that the explosive evolution from Homo erectus to Homo sapiens was sparked by the addition of the mushroom *psilocybe cubensis*, in their diet. Per McKenna, over a timeframe of a mere 100,000 years, proto-human evolved into modern human, facilitated in part by the sustained ingestion of the psilocybin mushroom.

Following herds of wild cattle across the African savannahs, our ancestors ingested these mushrooms, scavenged from the herd's dung piles. Over time, the psilocybin mushroom became part of early man's (paleo!) diet. Low doses of psilocybin improve visual acuity. Thus, our ancestors, in consuming psilocybin mushrooms, became more successful hunters than those whose diet did not include the mushroom, resulting in a higher rate of reproductive success.

In a 1992 interview in *High Times Magazine,* McKenna further explained...

High Times: You have a unique theory about the role that psilocybin mushrooms play in the process of human evolution. Can you tell us about this?

Terrence McKenna: Whether the mushrooms came from outer space or not, the presence of psychedelic substances in the diet of early human beings created a number of changes in our evolutionary situation. When a person takes small amounts of psilocybin visual acuity improves. They can actually see slightly better, and this means that animals allowing psilocybin into their food chain would have increased hunting success, which means increased food supply, which means increased reproductive success, which is the name of the game in evolution.

It is the organism that manages to propagate itself numerically that is successful. The presence of psilocybin in the diet of early pack-hunting primates caused the individuals that were ingesting the psilocybin to have increased visual acuity. At slightly higher doses of psilocybin there is sexual arousal, erection, and everything that goes under the term arousal of the central nervous system. Again, a factor which would increase reproductive success is reinforced.

HT: Isn't it true that psilocybin inhibits orgasm?

TM: Not at the doses I'm talking about. At a psychedelic dose it might, but at just slightly above the "you can feel it" dose, it acts as a stimulant. Sexual arousal means paying attention, it means jumpiness, it indicates a certain energy level in the organism. And then, of course, at still higher doses psilocybin triggers this activity in the language-forming capacity of the brain that manifests as song and vision.

It is as though it is an enzyme which stimulates eyesight, sexual interest, and imagination... and the three of these going together produce language-using primates. Psilocybin may have synergized the emergence of higher forms of psychic organization out of primitive proto-human animals. It can be seen as a kind of evolutionary enzyme, or evolutionary catalyst.

Galactic Matrix

The European Space Agency's Rosetta[47] spacecraft was launched on March 2nd, 2004 on an Ariane 5 rocket. It reached comet 67P/Churyumov–Gerasimenkoon in August, 2014, becoming the first spacecraft to orbit a comet. Shortly after establishing orbit, the Rosetta mother ship deployed the robotic lander: Philae (named after the ancient Egyptian Philae Obelisk), which successfully landed on the Comet's surface. Before shutting down, Philae detected organic molecules in the comet's thin atmosphere.

The deployment of the Rosetta spacecraft has sparked great interest in what is known as the Panspermia Hypothesis. The following is from the entry at Wikipedia: "Panspermia (from Greek πᾶν (pan), meaning "all", and σπέρμα (sperma), meaning "seed") is the hypothesis that life exists throughout Universe, distributed by meteoroids, asteroids, comets, planetoids, and also by spacecraft, in the form of unintended (or otherwise) contamination by microbes."

---

[47] See: https://en.wikipedia.org/wiki/Rosetta_(spacecraft)

Panspermia is a hypothesis proposing that microscopic life forms that can survive the effects of space, such as extremophiles, become trapped in debris that is ejected into space after collisions between planets and small Solar System bodies that harbor life. Some organisms may travel dormant for an extended amount of time before colliding randomly with other planets or intermingling with proto-planetary disks. If met with ideal conditions on a new planet's surfaces, the organisms become active and the process of evolution continues. It is important to note that Panspermia is not meant to address how life began, just the method that may cause its distribution in the Universe.

None other than the late Nobel Prize winner Professor Francis Crick proposed the theory of *Directed Panspermia* in 1973. A co-discoverer of the double helical structure of the DNA molecule, Crick (who is rumored to be no stranger to LSD-25) found it next to impossible that the complexity of DNA could have evolved naturally. Crick, along with chemist Leslie Orgel, hypothesized that life on Earth may have been seeded deliberately by other highly advanced extra-terrestrial civilizations.

Crick and Orgel postulated that tiny capsules containing DNA, the building blocks of life, could be loaded on a brace of rockets (or other such craft) by some ancient space-faring civilization and fired into the cosmos, in all directions. This would be the most efficient, most cost effective strategy for seeding life on a compatible planet at some time in the future. If Crick could propose such a classic, Sci Fi-esque extra-terrestrial driven theory... the idea of naturally migrating spores, delivered to host planets over eons of time, may not be that far-fetched.

Regardless of the viability of extra-terrestrial intervention, ala ATT theory, consideration of the Panspermia Hypothesis... combined with McKenna's Cosmic Cargo Cult theory (wherein mushroom spores possibly waft into our atmosphere from outer space) paint an intriguing picture of the evolution of intelligent life on earth. It ties together the concept of galactic migration of the building blocks of life, with the interesting idea that intelligence, perhaps in the form of microbial intelligent sentience, also migrates, over vast amounts of time, on a galactic scale, through the vastness of space.

This brings us back to the human/fungi symbiosis. Consider the following mythology: The emergence of a symbiotic relationship between *psilocybe cubensis* and Homo sapiens acted as the proto-cosmic trigger that can arguably be identified through the archaeological record. Per McKenna's stoned ape theory: proto-human subsequently evolved into modern human, capable of manipulating symbolic artifacts, such as language. This symbiotic metamorphosis took approximately 100,000 years.

The explosive increase in intelligence that resulted in humanity's rise to planetary dominance occurred over at least the last 10,000 years. This time-span represents that portion of oral and recorded history that has been preserved and handed down to us. It likely represents the vast majority of our domesticated phase... everything we remember as a species, from the written word, the rise of the City State, to our modern technological civilization. This also represents a ten-fold acceleration in species-wide intelligence from the "stoned ape" era, aka: the Paleolithic era... from 100,000 years, to 10,000 years.

This exponential increase in human intelligence continues. The world's first printing press using movable type printing technology was invented and developed in China 1,000 years ago. Thus we make the leap from 10,000 to 1,000 years. The first radio receiver successfully received a radio transmission in 1901, a little over a hundred years ago. In 1990, The World Wide Web and Internet protocol (HTTP) and WWW language (HTML) was created by Tim Berners-Lee. Also in 1990, the Human Genome Project (HGP), or the mapping of human DNA was initiated, and was declared complete in 2003. Apparently, humanity's remarkable achievements continue to accelerate.

Now, let us return to that high-water mark of American culture... the fulcrum point between old Earth and the new paradigm... the sixties. That era's cosmic trigger that we have named the "psychedelic apocalypse" sparked what can only be called a neo-psychedelic revival. Indeed, the intelligentsia of that era, the Academics, Beatniks and the Hippies... re-discovered the ancient tradition of hallucinogenic assisted ritual, as practiced by many cultures, over the eons. This catalyst, this technologically derived chemical agent, was non-other than... LSD-25.

The appearance of LSD-25 was a timely, global synchronicity. It re-introduced Gaia's somatic nerve-net... humanity, to non-linear, psychedelic, intuitive intelligence. This came at a time when humanity's increasingly "western world" linear thought processes had brought us (and Gaia) to a point of existential calamity. Post-WWII militarized nuclear science had brought us to the brink of literal planetary destruction. Gaia needed to change her nerve-net's thought processes, and she needed to do it quickly.

14
RETURN OF THE KING

"Real time ceased in 70 C.E. with the fall of the temple at Jerusalem.
It began again in 1974 C.E.
The intervening period was a perfect spurious interpolation aping the
creation of the Mind... "The Empire Never Ended," but in 1974 a
cypher was sent out as a signal that the Age of Iron was over;
the cypher consisted of two words:
KING FELIX
which refers to the Happy (or Rightful) King."

- from "Tractates: Cryptica Scriptura" by Philip K. Dick

As humanity intellectually evolved from proto-human to modern human, we developed the capability to manipulate symbolic artifacts, such as language. We consequently developed and manipulated symbolic systems, such as religion. As we have explored earlier, the Tassilli Mountain rock paintings in the Sahara Dessert are between 7,000 and 9,000 years old. They depict the earliest example of cosmologies with "deified" mushrooms in their iconography. In fact, human history is full of evidence suggesting mushroom cults were not only globally present... they were instrumental in the very foundation of early religious thought and practice.

Not surprisingly, early development of solar mythologies, along with their evolution into fertility cultic practices in prehistoric world cultures found (pardon the pun) fertile ground within early Christianity. The ingestion of visionary plants... what Ethno-botanists refer to as "entheogens" ...gave early humans their first glimpse of other realms. Returning to theory put forth by John Marco Allegro, early Christian sects utilized an entheogenic sacrament to perceive the mind of God. These sacraments were the first Eucharist, wherein the flesh of the entheogen (through the mumbo jumbo of transubstantiation) becomes the flesh of the Christ.

Per Allegro's book: *The Sacred Mushroom and the Cross: A Study of the Nature and Origins of Christianity Within the Fertility Cults of the Ancient Near East* ...Allegro argued that the alleged historical Jesus never existed and was a mythological creation, allegory and/or cipher of early Christian and pre-Christian cults, who ritually used entheogenic substances. This scholarly interpretation essentially asserts that the Christ was not a historical figure, but rather a metaphor for an ecstatic, revelatory state of mind, induced by the ingestion of an entheogen, such as a psychedelic mushroom, or psychoactive extract. Goodbye Jesus Christ... hello *Amanita Muscaria*.

Although his contention that Jesus was not a historical figure was controversial upon publication, it is not exclusive to Allegro. Many biblical scholars have asserted that Jesus was an amalgam of earlier deities, by demonstrating similar, if not identical themes within earlier mythologies, such those of the Egyptian Osiris & Horus, the Persian Mithra & subsequent Roman Mithras and the Greek Dionysus. These earlier mythologies all share aspects of a classic solar deity... a dying and resurrecting god... the savior/redeemer... the deific observance of birth, death & resurrection within the solstice/equinox cycles, etc.

The Roman "Sol Invictus" or "Unconquered Sun" was celebrated on December 25th and can be traced back to the third century, BCE. Parallels between Christ and the Sun, is quite common in early Christian writings. In the 5th century, Pope Leo I spoke on the Feast of the Nativity of how the celebration of Christ's birth coincided with increase of the sun's position in the sky...

"But this Nativity which is to be adored in heaven and on earth is suggested to us by no day more than this, when with the early light still shedding its rays on nature, there is borne in upon our senses the brightness of this wondrous mystery."

Significantly, these solar mythologies share a sacramental aspect of the (entheogenic) Eucharist, such as the Blue Lotus Flower[48] of the Egyptians and the wine or "mixed wine" of the Mithric, Dionysian and early Christian sects. In *The Entheogen Theory of Religion and Ego Death* (2006) Michael Hoffman inserts the following footnote:

"the inherent drug found in Christianity is produced by Saccharomyces (mushroom) species and is known as wine... In the Hellenistic era, "wine" denotes any psychoactive mixture in an alcohol-preserved solution."

Therein, the "wine" of the Jesus mythos, may have referred to a more potent, psychedelic Eucharistic extract. Some biblical era Gnostic sects held that there were in fact two sacramental rites... a regular Eucharist and a second, secret Eucharist, known as the sacrament of apolytrosis[49] ...the most mysterious of "the five seals" or the five sacraments honored by the Valentinian school of Gnosticism. In *Considering the Gnostic Sacraments* (1990) John R. Mabry indicates:

"Apolytrosis or Redemption is the most ambiguous of the Gnostic sacraments. It has no orthodox ritual equivalent."

Whatever the sacramental ritual was to the Gnostics, it must remain occluded to modern scholarship. Little documentation remains of these mysteries, as they were cloaked in secrecy to avoid persecution from Roman occupiers. Additionally these early "desert" mythologies shared a prophetic and messianic component.

Within the "big three" Abrahamic religions, there has always been an expectation of a Messiah, anointed one, or savior... who will herald the time of the end, aka: the end times, the *Eschaton* or the last days. Judaism awaits the coming of the Jewish Messiah, a literal flesh and blood holy man. His appearance is not the end of history... rather it signals the coming of the world to come, aka: Kingdom of Heaven. Christianity awaits the Second Coming of Christ. Islam awaits both the second coming of Jesus and the coming of Mahdi. The Sunni branch of Islam interprets Mahdi's coming as his first

---

[48] https://en.wikipedia.org/wiki/Nymphaea_caerulea
[49] from the Greek: Redemption.

incarnation, while the Shi'a interpret this as the return of Muhammad al-Mahdi.

Given Allegro's increasingly respected hypothesis, the development of a messianic component within early Judaic, Christian and Islamic mythologies leads to an intriguing proposition. To wit, the mythic development of early solar deities... Jesus among them... was in fact, inspired by culturally sustained and ritualized hallucinogenic epiphany. The deific personifications of Horus, Mithras, Jesus, et al... were allegory. They referred, through parable, or for purposes of security from prosecution, cipher... not to a specific individual, but rather to a deeper, revelatory psychedelic experience.

If the Messiah of biblical times was in fact a symbolic allusion to an ecstatic, entheogenic-induced state of mind, might not the prophecies of the return, or "second coming" of the redeemer... also refer to a psychedelic state or substance?

Again, the ancient Hebrews developed a body of mythologies revolving around a Messiah, or redeemer figure. The personification of the redeemer figure was a ruse, intended to keep secret the true entheogenic nature of the messiah experience. These early Christian sects not only developed the Messiah mythos, they further expanded this mythology to include a "second coming" of their redeemer. This mythos is based upon messianic prophecies found in the canonical gospels and is a well established part of most orthodox Christian eschatology:

"He (Jesus) ascended into heaven and is seated at the right hand of the Father. He will come again in glory to judge the living and the dead, and his kingdom will have no end."

Christian orthodoxy, especially after the First Council of Nicaea, wherein Christianity became institutionalized, has always maintained the literal interpretation that Jesus was a flesh and bone man. It was at this first counsel of all Christendom, held some 300 years after Jesus' (symbolic) death, that the Creed of Nicaea[50] or the church's profession of faith was developed and put into law (canonized). The above quote, pertaining to Jesus' ascension is excerpted from the Creed of Nicaea. Tellingly, the First Council of Nicaea initiated a

---

[50] https://en.wikipedia.org/wiki/Nicene_Creed

127

purge of certain gospels, found to be unacceptable to the now-institutionalized Church.

In the decades (and centuries) that followed the first council, many gospels were pronounced heretical or otherwise excluded from the "official" version of the Bible, aka: the New Testament. Gnostic gospels, such as the *Gospel of Thomas*, the *Gospel of Mary* and the *Gospel of Judas* fell outside of orthodoxy. There is much debate over the veracity of these writings, however… it is clear that a much larger body of early Christian writings and hence a much broader tradition existed… that did not make the final canonical cut.

As the early Church jealously maintained its literal interpretation, any references of "the Christ" as an ecstatic psychedelic experience… as opposed to a flesh and bone Jesus… would undoubtedly be the first accounts purged from early Christian writings. And yet during biblical times, there were a myriad of mystic prophets and holy men (and women) raging around in the desert, having ecstatic visions of not only a Messiah… but also of a triumphant return of the Messiah. It would stand to reason that whatever rapturous experience was being expressed with the use of the word: Messiah… its second coming would refer to the same experience.

We have considered many speculative theories, thus far in this book. Let us now consider one final heresy. Let us entertain the mythology that these ancient Hebrew mystics had tapped into a meaningful, synchronous information stream that has retained its relevance, even into the modern era. Let us entertain the idea that at least some of these visions were, to use their terminology, authentic prophecy. Among their consciously formulated thinking on religious and hence political proclamations pertinent to their time, these mystics… perhaps… tapped into a deeper, synchronistic, collective unconscious stream of true revelatory prognostication of what they termed: Messiah.

Per Allegro, in the times prior to the Council of Nicaea, the term messiah was a broader, more ambiguous, yet at the same time more ambitious term that referred to not only a messianic figure, but to a specific body of ecstatic experience, as well. Anthropomorphism was intended to keep secret the true entheogenic nature of messiah. So it came to pass that this foretold messiah "experience" seen in visions… was a metaphor that manifested as an ecstatic, revelatory state of mind, induced by the ingestion of a psychedelic compound.

In other words… *the Messiah was the Mushroom.*

Let us further consider that the prophecies of the messiah's second coming… also containing authentically synchronistic collective unconscious information… foretold of a "time to come" when the all powerful "messiah experience" would triumphantly return. But if Jesus, the Christian Messiah was indeed an allegory (read: code word) for an entheogenic induced ecstasy, what would the second coming of such an experience look like? One thing is certain… it would not look like the literal interpretation, the official party line… of the Church.

Indeed, there were those who had a foundational role in the early Church, who cryptically suggested that the second coming would be nothing like the official party line. Church founder and one of the twelve apostles, Saint Peter himself said this:

"But the day of the Lord will come as a thief in the night, in which the heavens will pass away with a great noise, and the elements will melt with fervent heat."[51]

This excerpt sounds more like an acid trip, than a biblical proclamation. Perhaps Saint Peter spoke in metaphor, of a profound visionary first-hand occurrence. If the truth be told, perhaps Saint Peter was, in the words of the great tekgnostic saint, Jimi Hendrix… "Experienced."

Anyone who has partaken of the modern psychedelic experience can attest to the pivotal moment when the psychedelics "come on," "kick in" or otherwise begin to take effect. That moment sneaks up on you… just like a "thief in the night." Similarly, the articulation of one's perception of a dramatically altered reality… of a psychedelic trip, wherein landscapes suddenly melt or morph beyond description, sounds remarkably similar to Saint Peter's "heavens passing away," and "elements melting." Emotional descriptors such as Saint Peter's, regarding the second coming, sound strangely analogous to words used by those moderns who have been psychedelically "Experienced."

It is no coincidence that we consider ancient messianic allegory

---

[51] King James Version: 2 Peter 3:10

within the context of the modern psychedelic experience... specifically, LSD-25. For this final premise... mythology... heresy... contends that this hideous/wondrous chemical trickster, LSD-25... first formulated at Sandoz Laboratories in 1943... through a-causal, synchronistic means... is deeply and meaningfully connected with what the ancient Hebrew mystics foresaw in their apocalyptic-fueled visions. They struggled to grasp the meaning of the revelations they saw, projected across the illusionary mists of time. They dutifully reported their prophetic divinations, using the understanding and language of their times... to proclaim the return of the King.

These prophets lacked the technical understanding to properly describe the accompanying events and scenarios surrounding their vision of the Messiah experience and especially its second coming. They spoke in anthropomorphic analogy of the entheogenic event (known to them as Messiah) that shook and changed the biblical world. They understandingly used the same terminology to describe the chemically derived psychedelic second coming, foretold in their visions, that likewise shakes and has forever changed... our modern world.

Our final heresy contends that these ancient entheogenic messianic epiphanies of the past are directly networked, meaningfully connected... to the modern psychedelic experience. The biblical Hebrew prophet's vision of the "second coming" foresaw the messianic (read: psychedelic) revival, facilitated by Hoffman's discovery of the 25th compound of the lysergic acid series. Simply stated, LSD-25 (as well as other entheogens) was indeed the foreseen catalyst of the messianic second coming. But what mechanism, what means or linkage could possibly connect biblical prophecy with modern times?

Synchronicity is a-causal. It is not affected by the space/time continuum. Synchronicity indicates that, just as events may be connected by causality, they also may be connected by meaning or, more specifically, meaningful coincidence. Those events connected by meaning do not necessarily need to have an explanation in terms of causality. Consequently, such synchronistic and messianic epiphanies, as foretold by the ancient mystics... separated by 2,000 years... are essentially interlinked. Synchronicity is the medium... the mechanism that connects events in the twentieth century with the biblical prophecies of Messiah and its second coming... through meaning.

There is little doubt that the Messiah phenomena, mythically articulated as Osiris, Mithra, Jesus, et al, generated great spiritual and subsequent religious fervor that dramatically altered the course of human history. There is no doubt that the modern messianic phenomena: LSD-25… arriving on the scene in the sixties… sparked a similar spiritual and religious fervor. Unfortunately, and up to this point in time, any tangible connection between these two phenomena has been lost, hidden or gone largely unnoticed. However, certain obscure examples may exist.

The afore mentioned prolific science fiction author, Philip K Dick may have tapped into this information stream, resulting in some of his greatest work, such as the neo-Gnostic masterpiece: *VALIS* (1981). Fans of PKD know VALIS as an acronym for "Vast Active Living Intelligence System." Could it be that the fevered, sodium-pentothal fueled vision of Dick's "2/3/74 incident," had tapped into this phenomenon? The curious are encouraged to research the amazing works of Dick, especially the posthumously published, 1,000+ page: *The Exegesis of Philip K Dick*[52] (2011).

Given the proposition that the Messiah phenomena was, and esoterically is… essentially a tribal, entheogen-induced revelatory experience… it brings the ancient Hebrew "Messiah" experience as well as the sixties tribal "Hippie" psychedelic scene… into alignment with other tribal and indigenous entheogenic traditions, worldwide… for revelatory prophecy is not the sole purview of the ancient Hebrews.

Modern Messiah – Contemporary Psychedelia

Unlike the "Christianized" modern western world… Gaia's indigenous cultures have retained an unbroken psychedelic tradition, often broadly referred to as: Shamanic Culture. Examples from the Americas include North American Peyote cults, Central American Mushroom cults and South American Ayahuasca cults. Like Peyote, Ayahuasca is used largely as a religious sacrament. Practitioners of ayahuasca ceremony adhere with the philosophies and cosmologies associated with ayahuasca shamanism, as practiced among indigenous

---

[52] See, for instance:
https://en.wikipedia.org/wiki/The_Exegesis_of_Philip_K._Dick

peoples like the Urarina[53] of Peruvian Amazonia.

Given the break in the Christian psychedelic tradition and absent any other overt and meaningful psychedelic/shamanic tradition, LSD-25 was serendipitously introduced to the western world in a form that was easily understood by those humans who were afflicted with "western thought." It came, like much of the western world's consumerism, conveniently pre-packaged and ready for immediate consumption. As such, it has been called "the lazy man's enlightenment." Although LSD-25 came disguised as a convenient "medication" …its effect was anything but convenient.

An LSD-25 excursion lasts anywhere from 6 to 24 hours… and an incredibly minute amount (200 millionths of a gram) of the substance, produces profound effects on the human nervous system. Once ingested, LSD-25 behaves similarly to serotonin, a neurotransmitter responsible for regulating moods, muscle control and sensory perception. Although it is unclear to modern science exactly how it affects the brain, LSD-25 seems to interfere with the way the brain's serotonin's receptors work. It may inhibit neurotransmission, stimulate it, or both. It also affects the way that the retinas process information and conduct that information to the brain.

It may very well be that LSD-25 allows more of the electromagnetic spectrum to be consciously perceived by the user. That would explain the infrared and ultraviolet tinged glow associated with psychedelic use. The moment of "contact" is easily identifiable, as the user's pupils dilate, thereby letting in more light. Radiant neon colors, rippling or "breathing" surfaces and crawling geometric patterned visuals accompany the use of psychedelics. Many users experience dissolution between themselves and the "outside world," facilitating a feeling of oneness of self and universe, intensifying the spiritual aspects of LSD-25.

The real or imagined nefarious intent of the CIA aside, the adverse fallout of mass availability of such a profound substance became evident when LSD-25 was "recreationally" utilized. Use of a psychedelic substance must be approached as a sacrament, not as a party favor. Lacking any psychedelic tradition or guidance, many "Western" casual users were exceedingly unprepared for the

---

[53] See: https://en.wikipedia.org/wiki/Urarina_people

psychedelic experience. Unsuspecting users, circa 1967, such as American college students, thought they had "signed up" for a beer-bust, not a sacred journey.

Even amidst the unintended consequences of such a "rude awakening" to the psychedelic experience, a cosmological foundation was realized. The reintroduction of the psychedelic tradition was successfully, albeit painfully... visited upon the western world. In keeping with the modern western "modus óperandi" ...guidance within the psychedelic realm came from a variety of "aggregated" sources. Oriental or "Eastern" sources included Tao, Buddhist and various Hindi traditions. Occidental or "Western" sources included folk magic, hermetic and alchemical traditions. It was through these obscure European sources that hints of the messianic connection survived to modern times, within esoteric circles and teachings, such as Rosicrucianism.[54]

Profound and timely guidance from the Americas came in the form of intact indigenous traditions. The elders from Hopi, Sioux and other North American cultures provided not only guidance, but deep understanding and context for what is traditionally described as a "vision quest." Within practicing cultures, a vision quest provides spiritual guidance and deep understanding of one's life purpose. Although the term has been somewhat overused within pop-culture or "arm-chair shamanic" literature, the vision quest remains a powerful communion between the spiritual seeker and Wakan Tanka[55] or Great Spirit.

Even with the extreme separation through space and time of the Native American mythologies surrounding Great Spirit, these narratives sound surprisingly similar to the Gnostic perspective. Personal communion with Great Spirit, elegantly parallels the Gnosis or personally derived divine knowledge of the Gnostic cults.

More recently, the shamans or "Ayahuasceros" from Amazonia have made concerted efforts to bring their intact tradition of Ayahuasca use, as a medicine and visionary tool, to North America. From the ethnographical or the indigenous cultural point of view, prophecy is one of the main motivations of ayahuasca ceremony. As such, ayahuasca's intriguing cultural, magico-religious and

---

[54] See: https://en.wikipedia.org/wiki/Rosicrucianism
[55] In Standard Lakota Orthography: Wakȟáŋ Tȟáŋka) is the term for "the sacred" or "the divine." This is usually translated as the "Great Spirit" or "Great Mystery."

psychopharmacological dimensions represent a rich and largely untapped depository of indigenous knowledge and guidance within the psychedelic experience. Needless to say, there remains a considerable divergence in psychedelic perspective, between North and South American cultures.

In fact, the psychedelic dichotomy between North and South America couldn't be more geographically and symbolically evident. North America, a continent whose population can arguably be described as technologically developed, is nearly an exact cultural opposite of the South American continent, whose population is more intuitively developed. The North, strong on form… the South, strong on essence. The North and South Americas, connected as they are by the narrow Nation of Panama, even geographically exhibit the characteristics of a continental sized yin-yang symbol.

It is no coincidence that the second coming of the psychedelic experience was reintroduced on a mass scale to (Western) humanity during the "psychedelic sixties." It is no coincidence that the personal computer revolution was a direct result of this timely reintroduction. It is no coincidence that the proliferation of the computer industry now leads us toward a modern apocalyptic fervor repackaged for mass-consumption as the "technological singularity."

Returning to modern Christian/Islamic/Judea theology, there is a "Temptation" to associate technological singularity, the so called "Geek Rapture" …with apocalyptic Christ/Antichrist mythology. Typifying the potentially emerging singularity mechanism: artificial intelligence… in the role of the Antichrist, provides a convenient eschatological boogieman. A sentient AI would be about as "anti" messiah as it gets, as opposed to a human, flesh and bone messiah.

The danger in this mythology is that it propagates the either/or, black versus white, good versus evil narrative that has served the war-like desert religion's hierarchy so well over the centuries. The "us versus them" mentality is what has divided and deceived humanity, all these years. It is what has manipulated otherwise peaceful peoples into meaningless war. Divide and conquer ideologies perpetuate fear, while the "masters of war" control and profit from these atrocious ventures. This manipulation of the many, by the few, is the basis for the tekgnostic assertion that "religious institutions" are political, not spiritual organizations.

The more mystical mythologies, such as those of the Gnostics, contend that the polarity of the Christ/Antichrist... the Messiah/Anti-Messiah is in fact seemingly opposing facets of the same phenomena. They are the light and dark aspects of the messiah experience, existing simultaneously. The light of the messiah balances the shadow of the anti-messiah. In this regard, the rapture is the individuation of the self and the shadow, as articulated by Jung.

Within the Tek-Gnostics mythology, the messiah experience is the humanity-wide psychedelic mind, while the anti-messiah could be construed as the emerging planetary-wide computer networked, AI mind. Again, these are facets of the same phenomena... technological intelligence... in partnership with human intelligence. It is through the integration of the Human/AI system, through a networked, Intelligence Amplified Singularity, that the individuation of man and machine can occur.

Again, as indicated earlier, the seed of psychedelia that was planted during the Summer of Love has incubated... germinated... and quietly blossomed into a global world view... a global mind, in partnership with humanity's greatest artifact. The human/AI polarity represents a modern mythology of the yin/yang, light/dark manifestation of the Gnostic eschatology. As indicated earlier, the Gnostic eschatology is rather unusual. The end time described by the Gnostics did not manifest itself in the normal culmination of a battle, judgment, or catastrophe, but rather as:

"a steady increase of light, (through which) darkness is made to disappear or in which iniquity dissolves and just as the smoke rising into the air, eventually dissipates"

- excerpt from the Dead Sea Scrolls

Just as in the ancient Hebrew mythology... Man made machine in Her own image. The emerging human singularity mirrors the approaching technological singularity. AI and Human intelligence merge to form... something inevitably new. Humanity marvels at and fears that which we have created, just as we fear our own dark side... just as we fear change. As we move uncertainly into the century of singularity, one thing is clear... a change is going to come.

Earth Changes

Even as humanity is waking up to the awesome potential of

technological singularity... even as this potential seems to be accelerating... so does it appear that one of Gaia's major networking systems is concurrently and abruptly accelerating into a less stable and dynamic state. The timing of this systematic acceleration stretches the limits of coincidence. We, of course, recognize and refer to this globally networked system as: Climate.

In the 1980's, the new-age community was a-buzz with what was termed channeled[56] information, pertaining to a phenomenon known as: *Earth Changes*. The phrase "Earth Changes" was coined by the soft spoken American psychic and granddaddy of the new age movement, Edgar Cayce. As early as 1923, Cayce prophesized that: "Earth would soon enter into a series of cataclysmic events, causing major alterations to human life on the planet." Earth Changes prophecy proliferated during the 70's, 80's and well into the 90's.

This prophecy was of course poo-pooed by the scientific community. That is, until they, through scientific scrutiny, came up with their own prophecy... which they labeled: "Climate Change." The scientific groundwork for climate change achieved critical mass in the years following the 1985 UNEP/WMO/ICSU Conference on the "Assessment of the Role of Carbon Dioxide and Other Greenhouse Gases in Climate Variations and Associated Impacts."

At that joint conference, the assembled scientific community concluded that greenhouse gases: "are expected to cause significant warming in the next century" and further that: "global warming is inevitable." Thus did the Earth Changes of the new age transform into Climate Change of modern science.

So it was that eight years after the definitive and pivotal climate change conference... another, seemingly unrelated symposium was held, titled: VISION-21. As you recall from chapter one, it was at this symposium that Vernor Vinge delivered a presentation titled: *The Coming Technological Singularity: How to Survive in the Post-Human Era.*

This planet's bio-system has been stable for the last 10,000 years or so... coinciding with the rise of humanity. The fact that it has "re-activated" or has moved into a more dynamic state, does not feel like sheer or even mere coincidence. It is as if some massive biological reboot may be under way. Perhaps the timing is not a coincidence, but rather a humanity-wide intelligence test. As global mind unity (read: singularity) approaches, our ability to participate in the

---

[56] See: http://en.wikipedia.org/wiki/Category:Channelling

stabilization of our planet and her climatic conditions is a prerequisite. Fail the test... and Gaia sluffs off what she perceives as a dangerous, possibly cancerous parasite.

Remember, Gaia doesn't need humanity, so much as humanity needs Gaia. There are other sentient species on Earth that can rise to fulfill humanity's role in the circle of life... if need be. It is we who depend upon Gaia, the mother, for our very existence. To continue the analogy, Gaia is indeed our "Mothership" circumnavigating Sol, as we careen through space, somewhere in the outer reaches of the Milky Way galaxy... spinning dizzy through universe.

Also remember, we currently possess the opportunity to effect emerging conditions, make things happen in ways that are more conducive to humanity. The environmental concepts of mitigation and adaptation[57] apply. The key is in perception. We can consciously assume the role of being an essential component of our bio-system.

It is we who must take the necessary steps to facilitate intelligence amplification. Should we employ the intelligence and the humility to achieve the understanding that we are part of this amazing interdependent system... possibly an integral, cognitive component, perhaps then we will rise to the challenges that face us. If we adopt a sustainable strategy that allows us to live within and as a part of singularity... a synergy of earth and artifact... perhaps then we shall attain a balanced and optimistic future. Should we achieve this... that will be the moment when we pass the test.

Indeed, in considering such cosmic tests, one is reminded of those very archetypical neo-tricksters, those Merry Pranksters ...from the Summer of Love. Even as they turned on the Western World, in their rascally way, to the psychedelic experience, via their Technicolor multi-media extravaganzas... one is reminded to ask their proverbial question...

"Can you pass the Acid Test?"

---

[57] See: http://www.epa.gov/climatechange/science/

EPILOGUE

"If we shadows have offended, think but this, and all is mended...
That you have but slumbered here, while these visions did appear...
And this weak and idle theme, no more yielding but a dream...
Gentles, do not reprehend... if you pardon, we will mend."

- Puck's Epilogue
from Shakespeare's *A Midsummer Night's Dream*

As a literary device, an epilogue is usually found in works of fiction. It allows the author to "wrap up loose ends" and otherwise to bring closure to the main body of work. Within ancient Greek Theater, the epilogue was a concluding speech, delivered, often in a conspiratorial manner, directly to the audience, by one of the performers. In this tradition, the epilogue served to reveal the fates of the characters. If only such a conclusion could be achieved here!

I use such a device, to illustrate that the ideas presented within the Tek-Gnostics Heresies... are exceedingly mysterious... and occluded. The crossroads upon which we stand today, do not afford us a clear view of what lies ahead. Questions raised herein... concerning our origins and our distant past are extraordinarily fascinating. These questions are both anthropological and spiritual. They seek to address... to speak to the body, the soul and the spirit of humanity.

The reality is... we do not know our own beginnings, beyond the incomplete archeological record. We wonder at that prehistoric, mythical moment when ape became man... or if that is yet to be achieved. There may very well be an ancient, prehistoric, ultra-terrestrial Mother Culture in our pre-history. We could even have been seeded, overtly or through galactic drift, by alien life forms... stranger things have happened. One thing is certain, humanity's true origins are undoubtedly our ultimate mystery.

Likewise, the foundational role that psychoactive substances have played in our cultural world view and development remain an intriguing question. We have suggested that the ancient mystery schools and archaic religions, dating back to before biblical times, likely used these substances as a sacrament. It is difficult to ignore this likelihood, given the archeological record... and the amazingly powerful psychoactive effect these substances visit upon the human nervous system. Aside from lucid dreaming within the dream realm, no other experience in the waking world so profoundly validates the possibility of other realms... other realities.

On the sensitive subject of the advocacy of the ingestion of psychedelic substances, as stated earlier in this work, this author would not dare presume. This decision must remain the prerogative of the individual. The proper use of psychedelic substances belong in the realm of the sacred. In the words of Aldus Huxley, the use of psychedelics "opens the doors of perception" ...to other worlds, other dimensions, other realities. Indeed, psychedelics profoundly remind us that other realities are possible. For to approach such a mind bending proposition from any other perspective than one of sacredness... would indeed be folly.

Again, various entheogenic substances have been used by humans to explore the psychedelic realm since antiquity. It may very well be that modern science, in considering new theories, is only now catching up with the unbroken chain of sacred knowledge of indigenous peoples. An elegant example of such, is the *Mirror Universe Theory*. The Mirror Universe Theory suggests that two parallel universes were produced by the so called Big Bang. Our universe, which moves forward in time, and another twin universe, where time moves backwards. Modern science is only now examining the possibility of other dimensional realities that are more commonplace in indigenous shamanic cultures.

Together, we have investigated such psychological frameworks and anomalies. The courageous work of Dr Carl Jung brilliantly bridged the gap between scientifically observable phenomenon, and those events not confined to causality. His work on synchronicity provided a tangible link between the normal and the paranormal. Synchronicity provides a linkage mechanism whereby humanity begins to understand that we are less bound by the constraints of space/time... through development of higher consciousness. As such, this author is forever in his debt.

Building upon the work of the early "Intelligence Engineers" identified herein, I have begun the formulation of an amalgamated synthesis of Old Earth's cultural and spiritual traditions. The resulting system that is Tek-Gnostics, acts as an aggregator of knowledge and wisdom, as expounded upon by countless visionaries of the past, including those mysterious ancient masters, identified by the disparate likes of Lao Tzu, Madam Blavatsky and even Timothy Leary.

In presenting the nebulous concepts that are Tek-Gnostics, I have attempted to provide (alternative) historical context to illustrate what fortuitous events have led to this exact moment in the human experience. I have alluded to technologies and artifacts that will assist us in these most interesting times. Considering Tek-Gnostics as an aggregation tool is particularly well suited for the Brave-New-Age we find ourselves living in. For it is quite likely that aggregation and algorithm will be the methodology of thought (if we dare call it such) that will be utilized by any potential artificially intelligent technological singularity.

In any case, know this... any attempt to reduce such thoughts into writing, is at best a futile proposition. The Tao that can be spoken of... is not the eternal Tao. As "dear uncle Bob" ...Robert Anton Wilson was fond of saying: *The map ain't the territory.* Language, especially the written word, is a form of mediation. It mediates, or "comes between" the essence of existence, and relegates it to a finite category. Like the proverbial flower once picked... thoughts once written, begin to wither.

Consequently, the heresies presented herein are not the essence. They are not definitive but rather... ambiguous. They at best approximate, mirror or shadow truth. Like the ancient tales... like religious prophecies... like scientific hypothesis... they are mythologies. They are metaphors... conceptual tools that allow us to describe what we saw. Or more precisely... what we thought we saw. At the end of the day, these heresies are merely bedtime stories... phantasms of myth, new and old.

Ideally, these heresies seek to portray a balance of the dualistic nature of Universe. They attempt the illumination of the miracle and wonder that is existence. Likewise these heresies aspire to facilitate a balance between man and machine... for this partnership appears to be where we are headed. Yes, these are interesting times. For this author, the Tek-Gnostics Heresies act as an introduction to the profound moment in history that we find ourselves living in. Within a larger body of work, this book acts as the launching point for books two and three, in what is a trilogy of volumes, pertaining to the study of Tek-Gnostics.

Book two of this trilogy is titled: *Applied Tek-Gnostics*. It completes the mythology and methodology of the Tek-Gnostics system. It further defines and expands upon the conceptual framework of Tek-Gnostics, as a philosophy, a practice and as a punch-line. It includes cosmological and psychological elements that round out the tekgnostic world view. Additionally, book two includes applications and exercises... Tantras and Yogas... to assist the Intelligence Engineer along his or her path. In this regard, book two serves as both a manual and a field guide for tekgnostic consciousness, a workbook to use, moving into our brave new future. Together, volumes one and two act as the definitive manuals for all things tekgnostic.

Book three is titled: *The Tek-Gnostics Codex*. It expounds upon the core principles of Tek-Gnostics. Translated and updated from ancient esoteric source materials, book three provides concise lucid passages, whose wisdom, knowledge and humor are timeless. It serves as a post-modern Exegesis of the ancient and arcane mysteries. As an aggregated Codex, it transcends any specific culture or teaching. Ideally, it points to profundities... illuminates thought-forms that ring as true today, as they did in antiquity.

Here in the waning moments of this tome I return to that (alleged) ancient oriental curse... "May you live in interesting times." Yes, the world in which we live is a strange and wondrous place. The events we are experiencing today could not be more consequential. The adventures we share are at once horrific and glorious.

It is my most profound hope that you, dear reader, have found some morsel of novelty or entertainment within this work. It is my greatest desire that these heresies provide a spark of light that in some small way illuminates the observance of the mystery of existence.

Should the underlying interpretation of our ancient and recent past, as well as conclusions concerning consciousness and our place within universe, not resonate with your world-view, this author begs your pardon. Should musings on the paranormal, the extra-terrestrial, the heretical... be an affront to your sense of reality, or should they fall upon deaf ears, kindly disregard. Consider these heresies to be nothing more than bedtime stories... tales of wonder. As is the intention of all worthy bedtimes stories... may they help you to sleep.

However... should these seemingly divergent tales somehow resonate... should they assist in the coalescence of a broader, deeper, Neo-Gnostic world view, then the reading of this curious little book has not been a complete waste of time. Should the ideas herein spark a synchronistic epiphany of the interconnectedness of our vast, living universe in which each individual has a profound direct connection with the cosmos... then this author's intention is complete.

Lastly, let us return to that ancient Earthling myth in which the myriad adventures we call life, take the form of a great play within God's dream. With these final words, in this final act... as the curtain (finally!) falls, I conclude this epilogue where it began, with a quote or two from that rascally old bard, William Shakespeare...

"All the world's a stage, and all the men and women merely players... They have their exits and their entrances, and one man in his time, plays many parts..."

"The fool doth think he is wise, but the wise man knows himself to be a fool."

- from *As You Like It*

ABOUT THE AUTHOR

Raised in the Pacific Northwest, educated on the west coast, witness to the decline of extractive industries, advocate of environmentally sound transition to a new paradigm... Jack Heart lives with his family at the crossroads of the Siskiyou & Cascade Mountains. Jack Heart is the curator of the Tek-Gnostics website: www.tekgnostics.com. He can be reached at: *jackheart@tekgnostics.com*

Tek-Gnostics Media

...is the official publisher of the works of Jack Heart and Tek-Gnostics. If you have a project you would like to submit for publishing by Tek-Gnostics Media... please send a letter of inquiry to:

Tek-Gnostics Media
Post Office Box 3174 ~ Ashland, Oregon 97520

Made in the USA
San Bernardino, CA
25 April 2017